T0032857

Investing
in Stocks

by Paul Mladjenovic

for
dummies®
A Wiley Brand

Investing in Stocks For Dummies®

Published by: **John Wiley & Sons, Inc.**, 111 River Street, Hoboken, NJ 07030-5774, www.wiley.com

Copyright © 2023 by John Wiley & Sons, Inc., Hoboken, New Jersey

Published simultaneously in Canada

For general information on our other products and services, please contact our Customer Care Department within the U.S. at 877-762-2974, outside the U.S. at 317-572-3993, or fax 317-572-4002. For technical support, please visit https://hub.wiley.com/community/support/dummies.

Wiley publishes in a variety of print and electronic formats and by print-on-demand. Some material included with standard print versions of this book may not be included in e-books or in print-on-demand. If this book refers to media such as a CD or DVD that is not included in the version you purchased, you may download this material at http://booksupport.wiley.com. For more information about Wiley products, visit www.wiley.com.

Library of Congress Control Number: 2023938989

ISBN 978-1-394-20113-6 (pbk); ISBN 978-1-394-20114-3 (ebk); ISBN 978-1-394-20115-0 (ebk)

SKY10053404_081623

Contents at a Glance

Table of Contents

Introduction

Successful stock investing takes diligent work and acquired knowledge, like any other meaningful pursuit. This book can definitely help you avoid the mistakes others have made and point you in the right direction. It gives you a heads-up about trends and conditions that are found in few other stock investing guides. Explore the pages of this book and find the topics that most interest you within the world of stock investing. Let me assure you that I've squeezed more than a quarter-century of experience, education, and expertise between these covers. My track record is as good as (or better than) the track records of many experts who trumpet their successes. More important, I share information to avoid common mistakes (some of which I made myself!). Understanding what not to do can be just as important as figuring out what to do.

In all the years that I've counseled and educated investors, the single difference between success and failure, between gain and loss, has boiled down to two words: *applied knowledge*. Take this book as your first step in a lifelong learning adventure.

About This Book

The stock market has been a cornerstone of the investor's passive wealth-building program for over a century and continues in this role. Recent years have been one huge roller-coaster ride for stock investors. Fortunes have been made and lost. With all the media attention and all the talking heads on radio and television, the investing public still didn't avoid losing trillions in a historic stock market debacle. Sadly, even the so-called experts who understand stocks didn't see the economic and geopolitical forces that acted like a tsunami on the market. With just a little more knowledge and a few wealth-preserving techniques, more investors could've held onto their hard-earned stock market fortunes.

Cheer up, though: This book gives you an early warning on those mega-trends and events that will affect your stock portfolio. Other books may tell you about stocks, but this book tells you about companies' performance and financial condition and how their stock prices are affected.

This book is designed to give you a realistic approach to making money in stocks. It provides the essence of sound, practical stock-investing strategies and insights that have been market-tested and proven from more than 100 years of stock market history. I don't expect you to read it cover to cover, although I'd be delighted if you read every word! Instead, this book is designed as a reference tool. Feel free to read the chapters in whatever order you choose. You can flip to the sections and chapters that interest you or those that include topics that you need to know more about.

Sidebars (gray boxes of text) in this book give you a more in-depth look at a certain topic. Although they further illuminate a particular point, these sidebars aren't crucial to your understanding of the rest of the book. Feel free to read them or skip them. Of course, I'd love for you to read them all, but my feelings won't be hurt if you decide to skip over them.

The text that accompanies the Technical Stuff icon (see the forthcoming section "Icons Used in This Book") can be passed over as well. The text associated with this icon gives some technical details about stock investing that are certainly interesting and informative, but you can still come away with the information you need without reading this text.

Investing in Stocks For Dummies is also quite different from the "get rich with stocks" titles that have crammed the bookshelves in recent years. It doesn't take a standard approach to the topic; it doesn't assume that stocks are a sure thing and the be-all, end-all of wealth building. In fact, at times in this book, I tell you *not* to invest in stocks (or even to bet against them!).

This book can help you succeed not only in up markets but also in down markets. Bull markets and bear markets come and go, but the informed investor can keep making money regardless. To give you an extra edge, I've tried to include information about the investing environment for stocks. Whether it's politics or hurricanes (or both), you need to know how the big picture affects your stock investment decisions.

One last note: Within this book, you may note that some web addresses break across two lines of text. If you're reading this book in print and you want to visit one of these web pages, simply key in the web address exactly as it's noted in the text, pretending as though the line break doesn't exist. If you're reading this as an e-book, you've got it easy — just click the web address to be taken directly to the web page.

Foolish Assumptions

I figure you've picked up this book for one or more of the following reasons:

>> You're a beginner and you want a crash course on stock investing that's an easy read.

>> You're already a stock investor, and you need a book that allows you to read only those chapters that cover specific stock-investing topics of interest to you.

>> You need to review your own situation with the information in this book to see whether you missed anything when you invested in that hot stock that your brother-in-law recommended.

>> You need a great gift! When Uncle Mo is upset over his poor stock picks, you can give him this book so he can get back on his financial feet. Be sure to get a copy for his broker, too. (Odds are, the broker was the one who made those picks to begin with.)

Icons Used in This Book

Useful icons appear in the margins of this book; here's what they mean.

REMEMBER

When you see the Remember icon, I'm reminding you about some information that you should always keep stashed in your memory, whether you're new to investing or an old pro.

TECHNICAL STUFF

The text attached to the Technical Stuff icon may not be crucial to your success as an investor, but it may enable you to talk shop with investing gurus and better understand the financial pages of your favorite business publication or website.

The Tip icon flags a particular bit of advice that just may give you an edge over other investors.

Pay special attention to the Warning icon because the advice can prevent headaches, heartaches, and financial aches.

Where to Go from Here

You may not need to read every chapter to make you more confident as a stock investor, so feel free to jump around to suit your personal needs. Because every chapter is designed to be as self-contained as possible, it won't do you any harm to cherry-pick what you really want to read. But if you're like me, you may still want to check out every chapter because you never know when you may come across a new tip or resource that will make a profitable difference in your stock portfolio. I want you to be successful so that I can brag about you!

1

Getting Started with Stock Investing

Brush up on stock basics, including how to calculate market capitalization and pick winners.

Find out what you should do before you invest your first dollar in stocks. Evaluate your current financial goals and situation.

Know the different approaches to stock investing and which approach may be right for you.

Figure out the risks of stock investing and discover the best ways around them. Understand the concept of volatility.

Chapter **1**

Introducing the World of Stock Investing

I think that there are great stock investment opportunities in virtually any time — even for newbies. There are great stocks to help you build your wealth (or provide dividend income) in both up and down markets. In fact, a *bear market* (a long period of falling prices) can be a great time to buy stocks because they're cheaper (think "sale!"). The key is knowing what to do (and even why), but that's what this book is for!

Today's stock market is a little puzzling, but it can still be rewarding. I can only promise that if you follow the advice in this book, you'll do *much* better than the average investor. Note that patience and discipline count now more than ever.

The purpose of this book is not only to tell you about the basics of stock investing but also to let you in on solid strategies that can help you profit from the stock market. Before you invest, you need to understand the fundamentals of stock investing, which I introduce in this chapter. Then I give you an overview of how to put your money where it will count the most.

Understanding the Basics

The basics of stock investing are so elementary that few people recognize them. When you lose track of the basics, you lose track of why you invested to begin with. This book helps you grasp these basics:

>> **Knowing the risk and volatility involved:** Perhaps the most fundamental (and, therefore, most important) concept to grasp is the risk you face whenever you put your hard-earned money in an investment such as a stock. Related to risk is the concept of volatility. *Volatility* refers to a condition in which there is rapid movement in the price of a particular stock (or other security); investors use this term especially when there's a sudden drop in price in a relatively short period of time. Find out more about risk and volatility in Chapter 4.

>> **Assessing your financial situation:** You need a firm awareness of your starting point and where you want to go. Chapter 2 helps you take stock of your current financial status and your goals.

>> **Understanding approaches to investing:** You want to approach investing in a way that works best for you. Chapter 3 defines the most common approaches to investing.

>> **Seeing what exchange-traded funds (ETFs) have to offer:** ETFs are like mutual funds, but they can be traded like stocks. I think that every stock investor should consider ETFs as a positive addition to their portfolio strategies. See Chapter 11 for the lowdown on ETFs.

REMEMBER

The bottom line in stock investing is that you shouldn't immediately send your money to a brokerage account or go to a website and click a Buy Stock button. The first thing you should do is find out as much as you can about what stocks are and how to use them to achieve your wealth-building goals.

Before you continue, I want to clarify exactly what a stock is. *Stock* is a type of security that indicates ownership in a corporation and represents a defined portion (measured in shares) of that corporation's future success. The two primary types of stocks are common and preferred:

>> **Common stock:** This type of stock, which I cover throughout this book, entitles the owner to vote at shareholders' meetings and receive any dividends that the company issues.

>> **Preferred stock:** This type of stock doesn't usually confer voting rights, but it does include some rights that exceed those of common stock. Preferred stockholders, for example, have preferential treatment in certain conditions, such as receiving dividends before common stockholders in the event of a corporate liquidation or bankruptcy. Additionally, preferred stock seeks to operate similarly to a bond for investors seeking stable income.

In this book, I mostly cover common stock. I also cover ETFs because they can be a valuable part of the stock investor's portfolio.

Preparing to Buy Stocks

Gathering information is critical in your stock-investing pursuits. You should gather information on your stock picks two times: before you invest and after you invest. Obviously, you should become more informed before you invest your first dollar, but you also need to stay informed about what's happening to the company whose stock you buy, as well as about the industry and the general economy. To find the best information sources, check out Chapter 5.

When you're ready to invest, you need to open a brokerage account. How do you know which broker to use? Chapter 8 provides some answers and resources to help you choose a broker. After you've opened a brokerage account, it pays to get familiar with the types of orders you can implement inside that account; find out more in Chapter 13.

Knowing How to Pick Winners

When you get past the basics, you can get to the meat of stock picking. Successful stock picking isn't mysterious, but it does take some time, effort, and analysis. And the effort is worthwhile because stocks are a convenient and important part of most investors' portfolios. Read the following sections and be sure to leapfrog to the relevant chapters to get the inside scoop on hot stocks.

Recognizing stock value

Imagine that you like eggs, and you're buying them at the grocery store. In this example, the eggs are like companies, and the prices represent the prices that you would pay for the companies' stock. The grocery store is the stock market. What if two brands of eggs are similar, but one costs $2.99 a carton and the other costs $3.99? Which would you choose? Odds are that you'd look at both brands, judge their quality, and, if they're indeed similar, take the cheaper eggs. The eggs at $3.99 are overpriced.

The same is true of stocks. What if you compare two companies that are similar in every respect but have different share prices? All things being equal, the cheaper price represents a better buy for the investor.

But the egg example has another side. What if the quality of the two brands of eggs is significantly different, but their prices are the same? If one brand of eggs is stale, of poor quality, and priced at $2.99 and the other brand is fresh, of superior quality, and also priced at $2.99, which would you get? You would take the good brand because they're better eggs. Perhaps the lesser eggs are an acceptable purchase at $1.99, but they're overpriced at $2.99.

The same example works with stocks. A poorly run company isn't a good choice if you can buy a better company in the marketplace at the same — or a better — price.

Comparing the value of eggs may seem overly simplistic, but doing so does cut to the heart of stock investing. Eggs and egg prices can be as varied as companies and stock prices. As an investor, you must make it your job to find the best value for your investment dollars. (Otherwise, you get egg on your face. You saw that one coming, right?)

Understanding market capitalization and stock value

You can determine a company's value (and, thus, the value of its stock) in many ways. The most basic way is to look at the company's market value, also known as market capitalization (or market cap). *Market capitalization* is simply the value you get when you multiply all the outstanding shares of a stock by the price of a single share. Calculating the market cap is easy; for example, if a company has 1 million shares outstanding and its share price is $10, the market cap is $10 million.

Small cap, mid cap, and *large cap* aren't references to headgear; they're references to how large a company is as measured by its market value. Here are the five basic stock categories of market capitalization:

>> **Micro cap (less than $300 million):** These stocks are the smallest and, hence, the riskiest available. (There's even a subsection of micro cap called *nano cap,* which refers to stocks under $50 million, but they're not appropriate for this book.)

>> **Small cap ($300 million to $2 billion):** These stocks fare better than the micro caps and still have plenty of growth potential. The key word here is *potential.*

>> **Mid cap ($2 billion to $10 billion):** For many investors, this category offers a good compromise between small caps and large caps. These stocks have some of the safety of large caps while retaining some of the growth potential of small caps.

>> **Large cap ($10 billion to $200 billion):** This category is usually best reserved for conservative stock investors who want steady appreciation with greater safety. Stocks in this category are frequently referred to as *blue chips.*

>> **Ultra cap or mega cap (more than $200 billion):** These stocks obviously refer to companies that are the biggest of the big. Stocks such as Google and Apple are examples.

REMEMBER

From a safety point of view, a company's size and market value do matter. All things being equal, large-cap stocks are considered safer than small-cap stocks. However, small-cap stocks have greater potential for growth. Compare these stocks to trees: Which tree is sturdier, a giant California redwood or a small oak tree that's just a year old? In a great storm, the redwood holds up well, whereas the smaller tree has a rough time. But you also have to ask yourself which tree has more opportunity for growth. The redwood may not have much growth left, but the small oak tree has plenty of growth to look forward to.

For beginning investors, comparing market cap to trees isn't so far-fetched. You want your money to branch out without becoming a sap.

REMEMBER

Although market capitalization is important to consider, don't invest (or not invest) based solely on it. It's just one measure of value. You need to look at numerous factors that can help you determine whether any given stock is a good investment. Keep reading — this book is full of information to help you decide.

Sharpening your investment skills

Investors who analyze a company can better judge the value of its stock and profit from buying and selling it. Your greatest asset in stock investing is knowledge (and a little common sense). To succeed in the world of stock investing, keep in mind these key success factors:

>> **Understand why you want to invest in stocks.** Are you seeking appreciation (capital gains) or income (dividends)? Turn to Chapters 9 and 10 for information on these topics.

>> **Timing your buys and sells does matter.** Terms like *overbought* and *oversold* can give you an edge when you're deciding whether to purchase or sell a stock. *Technical analysis* is a way to analyze securities through their market activity (past prices and volume) to find patterns that suggest where those investments may be headed in the short term.

>> **Do some research.** Look at the company whose stock you're considering to see whether it's a profitable business worthy of your investment dollars. Chapters 6 and 7 help you scrutinize companies.

>> **Understand and identify what's up with "the big picture."** It's a small world after all, and you should be aware of how the world can affect your stock portfolio. Everyone from the bureaucrats in Europe to the politicians in the U.S. Capitol can affect a stock or industry like a match in a dry haystack. Chapter 12 gives you lots of guidance on sector opportunities.

>> **Use investing strategies like the pros do.** I'm very big on strategies such as trailing stops and limit orders, and fortunately, today's technology gives you even more tools to help you grow or protect your money, so head on over to Chapter 13 for insights on ways to transact stock.

>> **Look outside the U.S. stock market for opportunities.** It's easier than ever before to profit from stocks offered across the globe! Find out more about investing in international stocks through American depositary receipts (ADRs) and international ETFs.

>> **Consider buying in smaller quantities.** Buying stocks doesn't always mean that you must buy through a broker and that it must be 100 shares. You can buy stock for as little as $25 using programs such as dividend reinvestment plans.

>> **Do as others do, not as they say.** Sometimes, what people tell you to do with stocks is not as revealing as what people are actually doing. This is why I like to look at company insiders before I buy or sell a particular stock. This includes insider trading done by Congress.

>> **Keep more of the money you earn.** After all your great work in getting the right stocks and making the big bucks, you should know about keeping more of the fruits of your investing. I cover taxes in Chapter 14.

Every chapter in this book offers you valuable guidance on some essential aspect of the fantastic world of stocks. The knowledge you pick up and apply from these pages has been tested over nearly a century of stock picking. The investment experience of the past — the good, the bad, and some of the ugly — is here for your benefit. Use this information to make a lot of money (and make me proud!).

Chapter **2**

Assessing Your Current Financial Situation and Goals

Y es, you want to make the big bucks. Or maybe you just want to get back the big bucks you lost in stocks during the *bear market* (a long period of falling prices) of the infamous global financial crisis of 2008–2009 or the lesser bear market of 2022. Either way, you want your money to grow so that you can have a better life. But before you make reservations for that Caribbean cruise you're dreaming about, you have to map out your action plan for getting there. Stocks can be a great component of most wealth-building programs, but you must first do some homework on a topic that you should be very familiar with — yourself. That's right. Understanding your current financial situation and clearly defining your financial goals are the first steps in successful investing.

Let me give you an example. I met an investor at one of my seminars who had a million dollars' worth of Procter & Gamble stock, and he was nearing retirement. He asked me whether he should sell his stock and become more growth-oriented by investing in a batch of *small-cap stocks* (stocks of a company worth $250 million to $1 billion; see Chapter 1 for more information). Because he already had enough assets to retire on at that time, I said that he didn't need to get more aggressive. In fact, I told him that he had too much tied to a single stock, even though it was a solid, large company. What would happen to his assets if problems arose at Procter & Gamble? Telling him to shrink his stock portfolio and put that money elsewhere — by paying off debt or adding investment-grade bonds for diversification, for example — seemed obvious.

This chapter is undoubtedly one of the most important chapters in this book. At first, you may think it's a chapter more suitable for some general book on personal finance. Wrong! Unsuccessful investors' greatest weakness is not understanding their financial situations and how stocks fit in. Often, I counsel people to stay out of the stock market if they aren't prepared for the responsibilities of stock investing, such as regularly reviewing the financial statements and progress of the companies they invest in.

REMEMBER

Investing in stocks requires balance. Investors sometimes tie up too much money in stocks, putting themselves at risk of losing a significant portion of their wealth if the market plunges. Then again, other investors place little or no money in stocks and, therefore, miss out on excellent opportunities to grow their wealth. Investors should make stocks a part of their portfolios, but the operative word is *part*. You should let stocks take up only a *portion* of your money. A disciplined investor also has money in bank accounts, investment-grade bonds, precious metals, and other assets that offer growth or income opportunities. Diversification is the key to minimizing risk. (For more on risk, see Chapter 4; I touch on volatility there, too.)

Establishing a Starting Point by Preparing a Balance Sheet

Whether you already own stocks or you're looking to get into the stock market, you need to find out about how much money you can afford to invest. No matter what you hope to accomplish with your stock-investing plan, the first step you should take is to figure out how much you own and how much you owe. To do this, prepare and review your personal balance sheet. A *balance sheet* is simply a list of your assets, your liabilities, and what each item is currently worth so you can arrive at your net worth. Your *net worth* is your total assets minus your total liabilities. (I know these terms sound like accounting mumbo jumbo, but knowing your net worth is important to your future financial success, so just do it.)

Composing your balance sheet is simple. You can use a spreadsheet program such as Microsoft Excel, or you can pull out a pencil and a piece of paper. Gather all your financial documents, such as bank and brokerage statements and other such paperwork; you need figures from these documents. Then follow the steps that I outline in the following sections. Update your balance sheet at least once a year to monitor your financial progress (is your net worth going up or down?).

TIP

Your personal balance sheet is really no different from balance sheets that giant companies prepare. (The main difference is a few zeros, but you can use my advice in this book to work on changing that.) In fact, the more you find out about your own balance sheet, the easier it is to understand the balance sheets of companies in which you're seeking to invest. (See Chapter 6 for details on reviewing company balance sheets.)

Step 1: Make sure you have an emergency fund

First, list cash on your balance sheet. Your goal is to have a reserve of at least three to six months' worth of your gross living expenses in cash and cash equivalents. The cash is important because it gives you a cushion. Three to six months' worth is usually enough to get you through the most common forms of financial disruption, such as losing your job.

REMEMBER

If your monthly expenses (or *outgo*) are $2,000, for example, you should have at least $6,000, and probably closer to $12,000, in a secure, Federal Deposit Insurance Corporation (FDIC)–insured, interest-bearing bank account (or another relatively safe, interest-bearing vehicle such as a money-market fund). Consider this account an emergency fund, not an investment. Don't use this money to buy stocks.

Too many Americans don't have an emergency fund, meaning that they put themselves at risk. Walking across a busy street while wearing a blindfold is a great example of putting yourself at risk, and in recent years, investors have done the financial equivalent. Investors piled on tremendous debt, put too much into investments (such as stocks) that they didn't understand, and had little or no savings. One of the biggest problems during this past decade was that savings were sinking to record lows while debt levels were reaching new heights. People then sold many stocks because they needed funds for — you guessed it — paying bills and servicing debt.

Resist the urge to start thinking of your investment in stocks as a savings account generating more than 20 percent per year. This is dangerous thinking! If your investments tank or you lose your job, you'll have financial difficulty, and that will affect your stock portfolio; you may have to sell some stocks in your account just to get money to pay the bills. An emergency fund helps you through a temporary cash crunch.

Step 2: List your assets in descending order of liquidity

Liquid assets aren't references to beer or cola (unless you're Anheuser-Busch InBev). Instead, *liquidity* refers to how quickly you can convert a particular *asset* (something you own that has value) into cash. If you know the liquidity of your assets, including investments, you have some options when you need cash to buy some stock (or pay some bills). All too often, people are short on cash and have too much wealth tied up in *illiquid* investments such as real estate. *Illiquid* is just a fancy way of saying that you don't have the immediate cash to meet a pressing need. (Hey, we've all had those moments!) Review your assets and take measures to ensure that enough of them are liquid (along with your illiquid assets).

Listing your assets in order of liquidity on your balance sheet gives you an immediate picture of which assets you can quickly convert to cash and which ones you can't. If you need money *now*, you can see that your cash in hand, your checking account, and your savings account are at the top of the list. The items last in order of liquidity become obvious; they're things like real estate and other assets that can take a long time to convert to cash.

Selling real estate, even in a seller's market, can take months. Investors who don't have adequate liquid assets run the risk of having to sell assets quickly and possibly at a loss as they scramble to accumulate the cash for their short-term financial obligations. For stock investors, this scramble may include prematurely selling stocks that they originally intended as long-term investments.

Table 2-1 shows a typical list of assets in order of liquidity. Use it as a guide for making your own asset list.

TABLE 2-1 Listing Personal Assets in Descending Order of Liquidity

Asset Item	Market Value	Annual Growth Rate
Current assets		
Cash on hand and in checking	$150	
Bank savings accounts and certificates of deposit (CDs)	$5,000	1%
Stocks	$2,000	11%
Mutual funds	$2,400	9%
Other assets (collectibles and so on)	$240	
Total current assets	**$9,790**	
Long-term assets		
Auto	$1,800	–10%
Residence	$150,000	5%
Real estate investment	$125,000	6%
Personal stuff (such as jewelry)	$4,000	
Total long-term assets	**$280,800**	
Total assets	**$290,590**	

Here's how to break down the information in Table 2-1:

>> **The first column** describes the asset. You can quickly convert *current assets* to cash — they're more liquid. *Long-term assets* have value, but you can't necessarily convert them to cash quickly — they aren't very liquid.

Note: I have stocks listed as short-term in the table. The reason is that this balance sheet is meant to list items in order of liquidity. Liquidity is best embodied in the question "How quickly can I turn this asset into cash?" Because a stock can be sold and converted to cash very quickly, it's a good example of a liquid asset. (However, that's not the main purpose for buying stocks.)

>> **The second column** gives the current market value for that item. Keep in mind that this value isn't the purchase price or original value; it's the amount you'd realistically get if you sold the asset in the current market at that moment.

>> **The third column** tells you how well that investment is doing compared to one year ago. If the percentage rate is 5 percent, that item is worth 5 percent more today than it was a year ago. You need to know how well all your assets are doing. Why? So you can adjust your assets for maximum growth or get rid of assets that are losing money. You should keep assets that are doing well (and you should consider increasing your holdings in these assets) and scrutinize assets that are down in value to see whether they're candidates for removal. Perhaps you can sell them and reinvest the money elsewhere. In addition, the realized loss has tax benefits (see Chapter 14).

TIP

Figuring the annual growth rate (in the third column) as a percentage isn't difficult. Say that you buy 100 shares of the stock Gro-A-Lot Corp., and its market value on December 31, 2021, is $50 per share for a total market value of $5,000 (100 shares × $50 per share). When you check its value on December 31, 2022, you find out that the stock is at $60 per share for a total market value of $6,000 (100 shares × $60 per share). The annual growth rate is 20 percent. You calculate this percentage by taking the amount of the gain ($60 per share – $50 per share = $10 gain per share), which is $1,000 (100 shares × the $10 gain), and dividing it by the value at the beginning of the time period ($5,000). In this case, you get 20 percent ($1,000 ÷ $5,000).

TIP

What if Gro-A-Lot Corp. stock also generates a dividend of $2 per share during that period? Now what? In that case, it generates a total return of 24 percent. To calculate the total return, add the appreciation ($10 per share × 100 shares = $1,000) and the dividend income ($2 per share × 100 shares = $200) and divide that sum ($1,000 + $200 = $1,200) by the value at the beginning of the year ($50 per share × 100 shares = $5,000). The total return is $1,200 on the $5,000 market value, or 24 percent.

>> **The last line** lists the total for all the assets and their current market value.

Step 3: List your liabilities

Liabilities are simply the bills that you're obligated to pay — your debt. Whether it's a credit card bill or a mortgage payment, a liability is an amount of money you have to pay back eventually (usually with interest). If you don't keep track of your liabilities, you may end up thinking that you have more money than you really do.

Table 2-2 lists some common liabilities. Use it as a model when you list your own. You should list the liabilities according to how soon you need to pay them. Credit card balances tend to be short-term obligations, whereas mortgages are long-term.

TABLE 2-2 ## Listing Personal Liabilities

Liabilities	Amount	Paying Rate
Credit cards	$4,000	18%
Personal loans	$13,000	10%
Mortgage	$100,000	4%
Total liabilities	**$117,000**	

Here's a summary of the information in Table 2-2:

REMEMBER

>> **The first column** names the type of debt. Don't forget to include student loans and auto loans if you have them.

Never avoid listing a liability because you're embarrassed to see how much you really owe. Be honest with yourself — doing so helps you improve your financial health.

>> **The second column** shows the current value (or current balance) of your liabilities. List the most current balance to see where you stand with your creditors.

>> **The third column** reflects how much interest you're paying for carrying that debt. This information is an important reminder about how debt can be a wealth zapper. Credit card debt can have an interest rate of 18 percent or more, and to add insult to injury, it isn't even tax-deductible. Using a credit card to make even a small purchase costs you if you don't pay off the balance each month. Within a year, a $50 sweater at 18 percent costs $59 when you add in the annual potential interest on the $50 you paid.

TIP

If you compare your liabilities in Table 2-2 and your personal assets in Table 2-1, you may find opportunities to reduce the amount you pay for interest. Say, for example, that you pay 18 percent on a credit card balance of $4,000, but you also have a personal asset of $5,000 in a bank savings account that's earning 2 percent in interest. In that case, you may want to consider taking $4,000 out of the savings account to pay off the credit card balance. Doing so saves you $640; the $4,000 in the bank was earning only $80 (2 percent of $4,000), while you were paying $720 on the credit card balance (18 percent of $4,000). Paying off your debt as soon as possible should always be your first consideration.

If you can't pay off high-interest debt, at least look for ways to minimize the cost of carrying the debt. The most obvious ways include the following:

>> **Replace high-interest cards with low-interest cards.** Many companies offer incentives to consumers, including signing up for cards with favorable rates (recently under 10 percent) that can be used to pay off high-interest cards (typically 12 percent to 18 percent or higher).

>> **Replace unsecured debt with secured debt.** Credit cards and personal loans are *unsecured* (you haven't put up any collateral or other asset to secure the debt); therefore, they have higher interest rates because this type of debt is considered riskier for the creditor. Sources of *secured debt* (such as home equity line accounts and brokerage accounts) provide you with a means to replace your high-interest debt with lower-interest debt. You get lower interest rates with secured debt because it's less risky for the creditor — the debt is backed up by collateral (your home or your stocks).

>> **Replace variable-interest debt with fixed-interest debt.** Think about how homeowners got blindsided when their monthly payments on adjustable-rate mortgages went up drastically in the wake of the housing bubble that popped during 2005–2008. If you can't lower your debt, at least make it fixed and predictable.

REMEMBER

Make a diligent effort to control and reduce your debt; otherwise, the debt can become too burdensome. If you don't control it, you may have to sell your stocks just to stay liquid. *Remember:* Murphy's Law states that you *will* sell your stock at the worst possible moment! Don't go there.

Step 4: Calculate your net worth

Your *net worth* is an indication of your total wealth. You can calculate your net worth with this basic equation: total assets (refer to Table 2-1) minus total liabilities (refer to Table 2-2) equal net worth (net assets or net equity).

Table 2-3 shows this equation in action with a net worth of $173,590 — a very respectable number. For many investors, just being in a position where assets exceed liabilities (a positive net worth) is great news. Use Table 2-3 as a model to analyze your own financial situation. Your mission (if you choose to accept it — and you should) is to ensure that your net worth increases from year to year as you progress toward your financial goals (I discuss financial goals later in this chapter).

TABLE 2-3 **Figuring Your Personal Net Worth**

Totals	Amounts	Increase from Year Before
Total assets (from Table 2-1)	$290,590	+5%
Total liabilities (from Table 2-2)	($117,000)	–2%
Net worth (total assets less total liabilities)	**$173,590**	**+3%**

Step 5: Analyze your balance sheet

After you create a balance sheet (based on the steps in the preceding sections) to illustrate your current finances, take a close look at it, and try to identify any changes you can make to increase your wealth. Sometimes, reaching your financial goals can be as simple as refocusing the items on your balance sheet (use Table 2-3 as a general guideline). Here are some brief points to consider:

>> **Is the money in your emergency (or rainy-day) fund sitting in an ultrasafe account and earning the highest interest available?** Bank money-market accounts or money-market funds are recommended. The safest type of account is a U.S. Treasury money-market fund. Banks are backed by the FDIC, while U.S. Treasury securities are backed by the "full faith and credit" of the federal government. Shop around for the best rates at sites such as www.bankrate. com, www.lendingtree.com, and www.lowermybills.com.

>> **Can you replace depreciating assets with appreciating assets?** Say you have two stereo systems. Why not sell one and invest the proceeds? You may say, "But I bought that unit two years ago for $500, and if I sell it now, I'll get only $300." That's your choice. You need to decide what helps your financial situation more — a $500 item that keeps shrinking in value (a *depreciating asset*) or $300 that can grow in value when invested (an *appreciating asset*).

>> **Can you replace low-yield investments with high-yield investments?** Maybe you have $5,000 in a bank CD earning 3 percent. You can certainly shop around for a better rate at another bank, but you can also seek alternatives that can offer a higher yield, such as U.S. savings bonds or short-term bond funds. Just keep in mind that if you already have a CD and you withdraw the funds before it matures, you may face a penalty (such as losing some interest).

>> **Can you pay off any high-interest debt with funds from low-interest assets?** If, for example, you have $5,000 earning 2 percent in a taxable bank account and you have $2,500 on a credit card charging 18 percent (which is not tax-deductible), you may as well pay off the credit card balance and save on the interest.

>> **If you're carrying debt, are you using that money for an investment return that's greater than the interest you're paying?** Carrying a loan with an interest rate of 8 percent is acceptable if that borrowed money is yielding more than 8 percent elsewhere. Suppose you have $6,000 in cash in a brokerage account. If you qualify, you can actually

make a stock purchase greater than $6,000 by using *margin* (essentially a loan from the broker). You can buy $12,000 of stock using your $6,000 in cash, with the remainder financed by the broker. Of course, you pay interest on that margin loan. But what if the interest rate is 6 percent and the stock you're about to invest in has a dividend that yields 9 percent? In that case, the dividend can help you pay off the margin loan, and you keep the additional income. (For more on buying on margin, see Chapter 13.)

>> **Can you sell any personal stuff for cash?** You can replace unproductive assets with cash from garage sales and auction websites.

>> **Can you use your home equity to pay off consumer debt?** Borrowing against your home has more favorable interest rates, and this interest is still tax-deductible.

Paying off consumer debt by using funds borrowed against your home is a great way to wipe the slate clean. What a relief to get rid of your credit card balances! Just don't turn around and run up your consumer debt again. You can get overburdened and experience financial ruin (not to mention homelessness). Not a pretty picture.

The important point to remember is that you can take control of your finances with discipline (and with the advice I offer in this book).

Funding Your Stock Program

If you're going to invest money in stocks, the first thing you need is . . . money! Where can you get that money? If you're waiting for an inheritance to come through, you may have to wait a long time, considering all the advances being made in health care lately. (What's that? You were going to invest in health-care stocks? How ironic.) Yet the challenge still comes down to how to fund your stock program.

Many investors can reallocate their investments and assets to do the trick. *Reallocating* simply means selling some investments or other assets and reinvesting that money into something else (such as stocks). It boils down to deciding what investment or asset you can sell or liquidate. Generally, you want to consider those investments and assets that give you a low return on your money (or no return at all). If you have a complicated mix of investments and assets, you may want to consider reviewing your options with a financial planner. Reallocation is just part of the answer; your cash flow is the other part.

Ever wonder why there's so much month left at the end of the money? Consider your cash flow. Your *cash flow* refers to what money is coming in (income) and what money is being spent (outgo). The net result is either a positive cash flow or a negative cash flow, depending on your cash management skills. Maintaining a positive cash flow (more money coming in than going out) helps you increase your net worth. A negative cash flow ultimately depletes your wealth and wipes out your net worth if you don't turn it around immediately.

The following sections show you how to calculate and analyze your cash flow. The first step is to do a cash flow statement. With a cash flow statement, you ask yourself three questions:

>> **What money is coming in?** In your cash flow statement, jot down all sources of income. Calculate income for the month and then for the year. Include everything: salary, wages, interest, dividends, and so on. Add them all up and get your grand total for income.

>> **What is your outgo?** Write down all the things that you spend money on. List all your expenses. If possible, categorize them as essential and nonessential. You can get an idea of all the expenses that you can reduce without affecting your lifestyle. But before you do that, make as complete a list as possible of what you spend your money on.

>> **What's left?** If your income is greater than your outgo, you have money ready and available for stock investing. No matter how small the amount seems, it definitely helps. I've seen fortunes built when people started to diligently invest as little as $25 to $50 per week or per month. If your outgo is greater than your income, you'd better sharpen your pencil. Cut down on nonessential spending and/or increase your income. If your budget is a little tight, hold off on your stock investing until your cash flow improves.

REMEMBER

Don't confuse a cash flow statement with an income statement (also called a *profit and loss statement* or an *income and expense statement*). A cash flow statement is simple to calculate because you can easily track what goes in and what goes out. Income statements are a little different (especially for businesses) because they take into account things that aren't technically cash flow (such as depreciation or amortization). Find out more about income statements in Chapter 6.

TIP

Consider treating regular, small stock investments as expenses in your budget. Many investors have made it a habit of paying $25, $50, or more per month into a dividend reinvestment plan so that they can conveniently build up a stock portfolio with relatively small amounts of money, and they do so with a disciplined approach.

Step 1: Tally up your income

Using Table 2-4 as a worksheet, list and calculate the money you have coming in. The first column describes the source of the money, the second column indicates the monthly amount from each respective source, and the last column indicates the amount projected for a full year. Include all income, such as wages, business income, dividends, interest income, and so on. Then project these amounts for a year (multiply by 12) and enter those amounts in the third column.

TABLE 2-4 **Listing Your Income**

Item	Monthly Amount	Yearly Amount
Salary and wages		
Interest income and dividends		
Business *net* (after taxes) income		
Other income		
Total income		

REMEMBER

Your total income is the amount of money you have to work with. To ensure your financial health, don't spend more than this amount. Always be aware of and carefully manage your income.

Step 2: Add up your outgo

Using Table 2-5 as a worksheet, list and calculate the money that's going out. How much are you spending and on what? The first column describes the source of the expense, the second column indicates the monthly amount, and the third column shows the amount projected for a full year. Include all the money you spend: credit card and other debt payments; household expenses, such as food, utility bills, and medical expenses; and nonessential expenses such as video games and elephant-foot umbrella stands.

TABLE 2-5 **Listing Your Expenses (Outgo)**

Item	Monthly Amount	Yearly Amount
Payroll taxes		
Rent or mortgage		
Utilities		
Food		
Clothing		
Insurance (medical, auto, homeowner's, and so on)		
Telephone/internet		
Real estate taxes		
Auto expenses		
Charity		
Recreation		
Credit card payments		
Loan payments		
Other		
Total outgo		

TIP

Payroll taxes is just a category in which to lump all the various taxes that the government takes out of your paycheck. Feel free to put each individual tax on its own line, if you prefer. The important thing is creating a comprehensive list that's meaningful to you.

REMEMBER

You may notice that the outgo doesn't include items such as payments to a 401(k) plan and other savings vehicles. Yes, these items do impact your cash flow, but they're not expenses; the amounts that you invest (or your employer invests for you) are essentially assets that benefit your financial situation versus expenses that don't help you build wealth. To account for the 401(k), simply deduct it from the gross pay before you calculate the preceding worksheet (Table 2-5). If, for example, your gross pay is $2,000 and your 401(k) contribution is $300, then use $1,700 as your income figure.

Step 3: Create a cash flow statement

Okay, you're almost to the end. The next step is creating a cash flow statement so you can see (all in one place) how your money moves — how much comes in and how much goes out and where it goes.

Plug the amount of your total income (from Table 2-4) and the amount of your total expenses (from Table 2-5) into the Table 2-6 worksheet to see your cash flow. Do you have positive cash flow — more coming in than going out — so that you can start investing in stocks (or other investments), or are expenses overpowering your income? Doing a cash flow statement isn't just about finding money in your financial situation to fund your stock program. First and foremost, it's about your financial well-being. Are you managing your finances well or not?

TABLE 2-6 **Looking at Your Cash Flow**

Item	Monthly Amount	Yearly Amount
Total income (from Table 2-4)		
Total outgo (from Table 2-5)		
Net inflow/outflow		

Watch your cash flow; keep your income growing and your expenses and debt as low as possible.

Step 4: Analyze your cash flow

Use your cash flow statement in Table 2-6 to identify sources of funds for your investment program. The more you can increase your income and decrease your outgo, the better. Scrutinize your data. Where can you improve the results? Here are some questions to ask yourself:

>> How can you increase your income? Do you have hobbies, interests, or skills that can generate extra cash?

>> Can you get more paid overtime at work? How about a promotion or a job change?

>> Where can you cut expenses?

>> Have you categorized your expenses as either "necessary" or "nonessential"?

>> Can you lower your debt payments by refinancing or consolidating loans and credit card balances?

>> Have you shopped around for lower insurance or telephone rates?

>> Have you analyzed your tax withholdings in your paycheck to make sure that you're not overpaying your taxes (just to get your overpayment back next year as a refund)?

Another option: Finding money to invest in tax savings

According to the Tax Foundation (https://taxfoundation.org), the average U.S. citizen pays more in taxes than for food, clothing, and shelter combined. Sit down with your tax advisor and try to find ways to reduce your taxes. A home-based business, for example, is a great way to gain new income and increase your tax deductions, resulting in a lower tax burden. Your tax advisor can make recommendations that work for you.

One tax strategy to consider is doing your stock investing in a tax-sheltered account such as a traditional individual retirement account (IRA) or a Roth IRA. Again, check with your tax advisor for deductions and strategies available to you. For more on the tax implications of stock investing, see Chapter 14.

Setting Your Sights on Your Financial Goals

Consider stocks as tools for living, just like any other investment — no more, no less. Stocks are among the many tools you use to accomplish something — to achieve a goal. Yes, successfully investing in stocks is the goal that you're probably shooting for if you're reading this book. However, you must complete the following sentence: "I want to be successful in my stock investing program to accomplish _____." You must consider stock investing as a means to an end. When people buy a computer, they don't (or shouldn't) think of buying a computer just to have a computer. People buy a computer because doing so helps them achieve a particular result, such as being more efficient in business, playing fun games, or having a nifty paperweight (tsk-tsk).

REMEMBER

Know the difference between long-term, intermediate-term, and short-term goals, and then set some of each (see Chapter 3 for more information):

>> **Long-term goals** refer to projects or financial goals that need funding five or more years from now.

>> **Intermediate-term goals** refer to financial goals that need funding two to five years from now.

>> **Short-term goals** need funding less than two years from now.

REMEMBER

Stocks, in general, are best suited for long-term goals such as:

>> Achieving financial independence (think retirement funding)

>> Paying for future college costs

>> Paying for any long-term expenditure or project

Some categories of stock (such as conservative or large cap) may be suitable for intermediate-term financial goals. If, for example, you'll retire four years from now, conservative stocks can be appropriate. If you're optimistic (or *bullish*) about the stock market and confident that stock prices will rise, go ahead and invest. However, if you're negative about the market (you're *bearish*, or you believe that stock prices will decline), you may want to wait until the economy starts to forge a clear path.

WARNING

Stocks generally aren't suitable for short-term investing goals because stock prices can behave irrationally in a short period of time. Stocks fluctuate from day to day, so you don't know what the stock will be worth in the near future. You may end up with less money than you expected. For investors seeking to reliably accrue money for short-term needs, short-term bank CDs or money-market funds are more appropriate.

REMEMBER

In recent years, investors have sought quick, short-term profits by trading and speculating in stocks. Lured by the fantastic returns generated by the stock market during 2009–2019, investors saw stocks as a get-rich-quick scheme. It's very important for you to understand the differences among *investing, saving,* and *speculating.* Which one do you want to do? Knowing the answer to this question is crucial to your goals and aspirations. Investors who don't know the difference tend to get burned. Here's some information to help you distinguish among these three actions:

>> *Investing* **is the act of putting your current funds into securities or tangible assets for the purpose of gaining future appreciation, income, or both.** You need time, knowledge, and discipline to invest. The investment can fluctuate in price, but you've chosen it for long-term potential.

>> *Saving* **is the safe accumulation of funds for a future use.** Savings don't fluctuate and are generally free of financial risk. The emphasis is on safety and liquidity.

>> *Speculating* **is the financial world's equivalent of gambling.** An investor who speculates is seeking quick profits gained from short-term price movements in a particular asset or investment. In recent years, many folks have been trading stocks (buying and selling in the short term with frequency), which is in the realm of short-term speculating.

These distinctly different concepts are often confused, even among so-called financial experts. I know of one financial advisor who actually put a child's college fund money into an internet stock fund, only to lose more than $17,000 in less than ten months! For more on the topic of risk, head to Chapter 4.

Chapter **3**

Defining Different Approaches to Stock Investing

"**I**nvesting for the long term" isn't just some perfunctory investment slogan from a bygone era; it's just as valid today as it was long ago. It's a culmination of proven stock-market experience that goes back many decades. Unfortunately, investor buying and selling habits have deteriorated in recent years due to impatience. Today's investors think that the short term is measured in days, the intermediate term is measured in weeks, and the long term is measured in months. Yeesh! No wonder so many folks are complaining about lousy investment returns. Investors have lost the profitable art of patience!

What should you do? Become an investor with a time horizon greater than one year (the emphasis is on *greater*). Give your investments time to grow. Everybody dreams about emulating the success of someone like Warren Buffett, but few emulate his patience (a huge part of his investment success).

Stocks are tools you can use to build your wealth. When used wisely, for the right purpose and in the right environment, they do a great job. But when improperly applied, they can lead to disaster. In this chapter, I show you how to choose the right types of investments based on your short-term, intermediate-term, and long-term financial goals. I also show you how to decide on your purpose for investing (growth or income investing) and your style of investing (conservative or aggressive).

Matching Stocks and Strategies with Your Goals

Various stocks are out there, as well as various investment approaches. The key to success in the stock market is matching the right kind of stock with the right kind of investment situation. You have to choose the stock and the approach that match your goals. (Chapter 2 has more on defining your financial goals.)

REMEMBER

Before investing in a stock, ask yourself, "When do I want to reach my financial goal?" Stocks are a means to an end. Your job is to figure out what that end is — or, more important, when it is. Do you want to retire in ten years or next year? Must you pay for your kid's college education next year or 18 years from now? The length of time you have before you need the money you hope to earn from stock investing determines what stocks you should buy. Table 3-1 gives you some guidelines for choosing the kind of stock best suited for the type of investor you are and the goals you have.

TIP

Dividends are payments made to a stock owner (unlike *interest*, which is payment to a creditor). Dividends are a great form of income, and companies that issue dividends tend to have more stable stock prices as well. (For more information on dividend-paying stocks, see the later section "Steadily making money: Income investing," as well as Chapter 10.)

REMEMBER

Table 3-1 gives you general guidelines, but not everyone fits into a particular profile. Every investor has a unique situation, set of goals, and level of risk tolerance. The terms *large cap, mid cap*, and *small cap* refer to the size (or *market capitalization*, also known as *market cap*) of the company. All factors being equal, large companies are safer (less risky) than small companies. (For more on market caps, see the later section "Investing for Your Personal Style," as well as Chapter 1.)

TABLE 3-1 Investor Types, Financial Goals, and Stock Types

Type of Investor	Time Frame for Financial Goals	Type of Stock Most Suitable
Conservative (worries about risk)	Long term (more than 5 years)	Large-cap stocks and mid-cap stocks.
Aggressive (high tolerance to risk)	Long term (more than 5 years)	Small-cap stocks and mid-cap stocks.
Conservative (worries about risk)	Intermediate term (2 to 5 years)	Large-cap stocks, preferably with dividends.
Aggressive (high tolerance to risk)	Intermediate term (2 to 5 years)	Small-cap stocks and mid-cap stocks.
Short term	1 to 2 years	Stocks are not suitable for the short term. Instead, look at vehicles such as savings accounts and money-market funds.
Very short term	Less than 1 year	Stocks? Don't even think about it! Well, you *can* invest in stocks for less than a year, but seriously, you're not really investing — you're either trading or short-term speculating. Instead, use savings accounts and money-market funds.

Investing for the Future

Are your goals long term or short term? Individual stocks can be either great or horrible choices, depending on the time period you want to focus on. Generally, the length of time you plan to invest in stocks can be short term, intermediate term, or long term. The following sections outline what kinds of stocks are most appropriate for each term length.

REMEMBER

Investing in quality stocks becomes less risky as the time frame lengthens. Stock prices tend to fluctuate daily but have a tendency to trend up or down over an extended period of time. Even if you invest in a stock that goes down in the short term, you're likely to see it rise and possibly exceed your investment if you have the patience to wait it out and let the stock price appreciate.

Focusing on the short term

Short term generally means one year or less, although some people extend the period to two years or less. Short-term investing isn't about making a quick buck on your stock choices — it refers to when you may need the money.

Every person has short-term goals. Some are modest, such as setting aside money for a vacation next month or paying for medical bills. Other short-term goals are more ambitious, such as accruing funds for a down payment to purchase a new home within six months. Whatever the expense or purchase, you need a predictable accumulation of cash soon. If this sounds like your situation, stay away from the stock market!

WARNING

Because stocks can be so unpredictable in the short term, they're a bad choice for short-term considerations. I get a kick out of market analysts on TV saying things such as, "At $25 a share, XYZ is a solid investment, and we feel that its stock should hit our target price of $40 within six to nine months." You know an eager investor hears that and says, "Gee, why bother with 1 percent at the bank when this stock will rise by more than 50 percent? I'd better call my broker." It may hit that target amount (or surpass it), or it may not. Most of the time, the stock doesn't reach the target price, and the investor is disappointed. The stock may even go down!

The reason that target prices are frequently missed is that it's difficult to figure out what millions of investors will do in the short term. The short term can be irrational because so many investors have so many reasons for buying and selling that it can be difficult to analyze. If you invest for an important short-term need, you can lose very important cash quicker than you think.

TECHNICAL
STUFF

During the raging bull market of 2002–2007, investors watched as some high-profile stocks went up 20 percent to 50 percent in a matter of months. Hey, who needs a savings account earning a measly interest rate when stocks grow like that! Of course, when the 2008–2009 bear market hit and those same stocks fell 50 percent to 85 percent, a savings account earning a measly interest rate suddenly didn't seem so bad.

SHORT-TERM INVESTING = SPECULATING

My case files are littered with examples of long-term stock investors who morphed into short-term speculators. I know of one fellow who had $80,000 and was set to get married within 12 months and then put a down payment on a new home for him and his bride. He wanted to surprise her by growing his nest egg quickly so they could have a glitzier wedding and a larger down payment.

What happened? The money instead shrank to $11,000 as his stock choices pulled back sharply. Ouch! How does that go again? For better or for worse . . . uh . . . for richer or for poorer? I'm sure they had to adjust their plans accordingly. I recall some of the stocks he chose, and now, years later, those stocks have recovered and gone on to new highs.

The bottom line is that investing in stocks for the short term is nothing more than speculating. Your only possible strategy is luck.

REMEMBER

Short-term stock investing is very unpredictable. Stocks — even the best ones — fluctuate in the short term. In a negative environment, they can be very volatile. No one can accurately predict the price movement (unless they have some inside information), so stocks are definitely inappropriate for any financial goal you need to reach within one year. You can better serve your short-term goals with stable, interest-bearing investments like certificates of deposit (CDs) at your local bank. (Refer to Table 3-1 for suggestions about your short-term strategies.)

Considering intermediate-term goals

Intermediate term refers to the financial goals you plan to reach in two to five years. For example, if you want to accumulate funds to put money down for investment in real estate four years from now, some growth-oriented investments may be suitable. (I discuss growth investing in more detail later in this chapter.)

Although some stocks *may* be appropriate for a two- or three-year period, not all stocks are good intermediate-term investments. Some stocks are fairly stable and hold their value well, such as the stock of large or established dividend-paying companies. Other stocks have prices that jump all over the place, such as those of untested companies that haven't been in existence long enough to develop a consistent track record.

If you plan to invest in the stock market to meet intermediate-term goals, consider large, established companies or dividend-paying companies in industries that provide the necessities of life (like the food and beverage industry or electric utilities). In today's economic environment, I strongly believe that stocks attached to companies that serve basic human needs should have a major presence in most stock portfolios. They're especially well suited for intermediate investment goals.

Just because a particular stock is labeled as being appropriate for the intermediate term doesn't mean you should get rid of it by the stroke of midnight five years from now. After all, if the company is doing well and going strong, you can continue holding the stock indefinitely. The more time you give a well-positioned, profitable company's stock to grow, the better you'll do.

Preparing for the long term

Stock investing is best suited for making money over a long period of time. Usually, when you measure stocks against other investments in terms of five to (preferably) ten or more years, they excel. Even investors who bought stocks during the depths of the Great Depression saw profitable growth in their stock portfolios over a ten-year period. In fact, if you examine any 10-year period over the past 50 years, you see that stocks beat out other financial investments (such as bonds or bank investments) in almost every period when measured by total return (taking into account reinvesting and compounding of capital gains and dividends)!

Of course, your work doesn't stop at deciding on a long-term investment. You still have to do your homework and choose stocks wisely, because even in good times, you can lose money if you invest in companies that go out of business. Parts 2 and 3 of this book show you how to evaluate specific companies and industries and alert you to factors in the general economy that can affect stock behavior.

Because so many different types and categories of stocks are available, virtually any investor with a long-term perspective should add stocks to their investment portfolio. Whether you want to save for a young child's college fund or for future retirement goals, carefully selected stocks have proven to be a superior long-term investment.

Investing for a Purpose

When someone asked the lady why she bungee jumped off the bridge that spanned a massive ravine, she answered, "Because it's fun!" When someone asked the fellow why he dove into a pool chock-full of alligators and snakes, he responded, "Because someone pushed me." You shouldn't invest in stocks unless you have a purpose that you understand, like investing for growth or income. Keep in mind that stocks are just a means to an end — figure out your desired end and then match the means. The following sections can help.

Even if an advisor pushes you to invest, be sure that advisor gives you an explanation of how each stock choice fits your purpose. I know of a very nice, elderly lady who had a portfolio brimming with aggressive-growth stocks because she had an overbearing broker. Her purpose should've been conservative, and she should've chosen investments that would preserve her wealth rather than grow it. Obviously, the broker's agenda got in the way. (To find out more about dealing with brokers, go to Chapter 8.)

Making loads of money quickly: Growth investing

When investors want their money to grow (instead of just trying to preserve it), they look for investments that appreciate in value. *Appreciate* is just another way of saying *grow*. If you bought a stock for $8 per share and now its value is $30 per share, your investment has grown by $22 per share — that's appreciation. I know I would appreciate it.

Appreciation is also known as capital gain (*capital gain* is most commonly used when it comes to taxes) and is probably the number-one reason people invest in stocks. Few investments have the potential to grow your wealth as conveniently as stocks.

If you want the stock market to make you loads of money (and you can assume some risk), head to Chapter 9, which takes an in-depth look at investing for growth.

WARNING

Stocks are a great way to grow your wealth, but they're not the only way. Many investors seek alternative ways to make money, but many of these alternative ways are more aggressive than stocks and carry significantly more risk. You may have heard about people who made quick fortunes in areas such as commodities (like wheat, pork bellies, or precious metals), options, and other more-sophisticated investment vehicles. Keep in mind that you should limit these riskier investments to only a small portion of your portfolio, such as 5 percent or 10 percent of your investable funds. Experienced investors can go higher.

Steadily making money: Income investing

Not all investors want to take on the risk that comes with making a killing. (Hey, no guts, no glory!) Some people just want to invest in the stock market as a means of providing a steady income. They don't need stock values to go through the ceiling. Instead, they need stocks that perform well consistently.

If your purpose for investing in stocks is to create income, you need to choose stocks that pay dividends. Dividends are typically paid quarterly to stockholders on record as of specific dates. How do you know if the dividend you're being paid is higher (or lower) than other vehicles (such as bonds)? The following sections help you figure it out.

Distinguishing between dividends and interest

Don't confuse dividends with interest. Most people are familiar with interest because that's how you grow your money over the years in the bank. The important difference is that *interest* is paid to creditors, and *dividends* are paid to owners (meaning *shareholders* — and if you own stock, you're a shareholder because shares of stock represent ownership in a publicly traded company).

REMEMBER

When you buy stock, you buy a piece of that company. When you put money in a bank (or when you buy bonds), you basically loan your money. You become a creditor, and the bank or bond issuer is the debtor; as such, it must eventually pay your money back to you with interest.

Recognizing the importance of yield

When you invest for income, you have to consider your investment's yield and compare it with the alternatives. The *yield* is an investment's payout expressed as a percentage of the investment amount. Looking at the yield is a way to compare the income you expect to receive from one investment with the expected income from others. Table 3-2 shows some comparative yields.

TABLE 3-2 **Comparing the Yields of Various Investments**

Investment	Type	Amount	Pay Type	Payout	Yield
Smith Co.	Stock	$50/share	Dividend	$2.50	5%
Jones Co.	Stock	$100/share	Dividend	$4	4%
Acme Bank	Bank CD	$500	Interest	$5	1%
Acme Bank	Bank CD	$2,500	Interest	$31.25	1.25%
Acme Bank	Bank CD	$5,000	Interest	$75	1.5%
Brown Co.	Bond	$5,000	Interest	$300	6%

To calculate yield, use the following formula:

Yield = Payout ÷ Investment amount

For the sake of simplicity, the following exercise is based on an annual percentage yield basis (compounding would increase the yield).

Jones Co. and Smith Co. are typical dividend-paying stocks. Looking at Table 3-2 and presuming that both companies are similar in most respects except for their differing dividends, how can you tell whether the $50 stock with a $2.50 annual dividend is better (or worse) than the $100 stock with a $4 annual dividend? The yield tells you. Even though Jones Co. pays a higher dividend ($4), Smith Co. has a higher yield (5 percent). Therefore, if you have to choose between those two stocks as an income investor, you should choose Smith Co. Of course, if you truly want to maximize your income and don't really need your investment to appreciate a lot, you should probably choose Brown Co.'s bond because it offers a yield of 6 percent.

Dividend-paying stocks do have the ability to increase in value. They may not have the same growth potential as growth stocks, but at the very least, they have a greater potential for capital gain than CDs or bonds. I cover dividend-paying stocks (good for investing for income) in Chapter 10.

Investing for Your Personal Style

Your investing style isn't a blue-jeans-versus-three-piece-suit debate. It refers to your approach to stock investing. Do you want to be conservative or aggressive? Would you rather be the tortoise or the hare? Your investment personality greatly depends on your purpose and the term over which you're planning to invest (see the previous two sections). The following sections outline the two most general investment styles.

Conservative investing

Conservative investing means that you put your money in something proven, tried, and true. You invest your money in safe and secure places, such as banks and government-backed securities. But how does that apply to stocks? (Refer to Table 3-1 for suggestions.)

If you're a conservative stock investor, you want to place your money in companies that exhibit some of the following qualities:

>> **Proven performance:** You want companies that have shown increasing sales and earnings year after year. You don't demand anything spectacular — just a strong and steady performance.

>> **Large market size:** You want to invest in large-cap companies — in other words, companies with a market value exceeding $5 billion to $25 billion. Conservative investors surmise that bigger is safer.

>> **Proven market leadership:** Look for companies that are leaders in their industries.

>> **Perceived staying power:** You want companies with the financial clout and market position to weather uncertain market and economic conditions. What happens in the economy or who gets elected shouldn't matter.

As a conservative investor, you don't mind if the companies' share prices jump (who would?), but you're more concerned with steady growth over the long term.

Aggressive investing

Aggressive investors can plan long term or look over only the intermediate term, but in any case, they want stocks that resemble jackrabbits — those that show the potential to break out of the pack.

If you're an aggressive stock investor, you want to invest your money in companies that exhibit some of the following qualities:

>> **Great potential:** Choose companies that have superior goods, services, ideas, or ways of doing business compared to the competition.

>> **Capital gains possibility:** Don't even consider dividends. If anything, you dislike dividends. You feel that the money dispensed in dividend form is better reinvested in the company. This, in turn, can spur greater growth.

>> **Innovation:** Find companies that have innovative or disruptive technologies, ideas, or methods that make them stand apart from other companies.

Aggressive investors usually seek out small capitalization stocks, known as *small caps*, because they can have plenty of potential for growth. Take the tree example, for instance: A giant redwood may be strong, but it may not grow much more, whereas a brand-new sapling has plenty of growth to look forward to. Why invest in big, stodgy companies when you can invest in smaller enterprises that may become the leaders of tomorrow? Aggressive investors have no problem buying stock in obscure businesses because they hope that such companies will become another Apple or McDonald's. Find out more about growth investing in Chapter 9.

Chapter **4**
Understanding Risk and Volatility

nvestors face many risks, most of which I cover in this chapter. The simplest definition of *risk* for investors is "the possibility that your investment will lose some (or all) of its value." Yet you don't have to fear risk if you understand it and plan for it. You must understand the oldest principle in the world of investing — risk versus return. This principle states the following:

> If you want a greater return on your money, you need to tolerate more risk. If you don't want to tolerate more risk, you must tolerate a lower rate of return.

This point about risk is best illustrated from a moment in one of my investment seminars. One of the attendees told me that he had his money in the bank but was dissatisfied with the rate of return. He lamented, "The yield on my money in the bank is pitiful! I want to put my money somewhere where it can grow." I asked him, "How about investing in common stocks? Or what about growth mutual funds? They have a solid, long-term growth track record." He responded, "Stocks? I don't want to put my money there. It's too risky!" Okay, then. If you don't want to tolerate more risk, don't complain about earning less on your money. Risk (in all its forms) has a bearing on all your money concerns and goals. That's why understanding risk before you invest is so important.

This man — as well as the rest of us — needs to remember that risk is not a four-letter word. (Well, it is a four-letter word, but you know what I mean.) Risk is present no matter what you do with your money. Even if you simply stick your money under your mattress, risk is involved — several kinds of risk, in fact. You have the risk of fire. (What if your house burns down?) You have the risk of theft. (What if burglars find your stash of cash?) You also have relative risk. (What if your relatives find your money?)

Be aware of the different kinds of risk that I describe in this chapter, so you can easily plan around them to keep your money growing. And don't forget risk's kid brother — volatility! Volatility is about the rapid movement in a short time frame (such as a single day) of buying or selling, which, in turn, causes stock prices to rise or fall rapidly.

TECHNICAL STUFF

Technically, volatility is considered a "neutral" condition, but it's usually associated with rapid downward movement of stock because that means sudden loss for investors and causes anxiety.

Exploring Different Kinds of Risk

Think about all the ways that an investment can lose money. You can list all sorts of possibilities — so many that you may think, "Holy cow! Why invest at all?"

Don't let risk frighten you. After all, life itself is risky. Just make sure that you understand the different kinds of risk in the following sections before you start navigating the investment world. Be mindful of risk and find out about the effects of risk on your investments and personal financial goals.

Financial risk

The financial risk of stock investing is that you can lose your money if the company whose stock you purchase loses money or goes belly-up. This type of risk is the most obvious because companies do go bankrupt.

You can greatly enhance the chances of your financial risk paying off by doing an adequate amount of research and choosing your stocks carefully (which this book helps you do — see Part 2 for details). Financial risk is a real concern even when the economy is doing well. Some diligent research, a little planning, and a dose of common sense help you reduce your financial risk.

In the stock-investing mania of the late 1990s, millions of investors (along with many well-known investment gurus) ignored some obvious financial risks of many then-popular stocks. Investors blindly plunked their money into stocks that were bad choices. Consider investors who put their money in DrKoop.com (a health information website) in 1999 and held on during 2000. This company had no profit and was over-indebted. DrKoop.com went into cardiac arrest as it collapsed from $45 per share to $2 per share by mid-2000. By the time the stock was DOA, investors lost millions. RIP (risky investment play!).

Internet and tech stocks littered the graveyard of stock market catastrophes during 2000–2001 because investors didn't see (or didn't want to see?) the risks involved with companies that didn't offer a solid record of results (profits, sales, and so on). When you invest in companies that don't have a proven track record, you're not investing, you're speculating.

Fast-forward to 2008. New risks abounded as the headlines railed on about the credit crisis on Wall Street and the subprime fiasco in the wake of the housing bubble popping. Think about how this crisis impacted investors as the market went through its stomach-churning roller-coaster ride. A good example of a casualty you didn't want to be a part of was Bear Stearns, which was caught in the subprime buzz saw. Bear Stearns was sky-high at $170 a share in early 2007, yet it crashed to $2 a share by March 2008 before disappearing in the dustbin of stock history. Yikes! Its problems arose from massive overexposure to bad debt. Investors could've done some research (the public data was revealing!) and avoided the stock entirely. The bear market of 2022 had its share of casualties, too.

Investors who did their homework regarding the financial conditions of companies such as the internet stocks (and Bear Stearns, among others) discovered that these companies had the hallmarks of financial risk — high debt, low (or no) earnings, and plenty of competition. They steered clear, avoiding tremendous financial loss. Investors who didn't do their homework were lured by the status of these companies and lost their shirts.

Of course, the individual investors who lost money by investing in these trendy, high-profile companies don't deserve all the responsibility for their tremendous financial losses; some high-profile analysts and media sources also should've known better. The late 1990s may someday be a case study of how euphoria and the herd mentality (rather than good, old-fashioned research and common sense) ruled the day (temporarily). The excitement of making potential fortunes gets the best of people sometimes, and they throw caution to the wind. Historians may look back at those days and say, "What *were* they thinking?" Achieving true wealth takes diligent work and careful analysis.

REMEMBER

In terms of financial risk, the bottom line is, well, the bottom line! A healthy bottom line means that a company is making money. And if a company is making money, then you can make money by investing in its stock. However, if a company isn't making money, you won't make money if you invest in it. Profit is the lifeblood of any company. (See Chapter 6 for the scoop on determining whether a company's bottom line is healthy.)

Interest rate risk

You can lose money in an apparently sound investment because of something that sounds as harmless as "interest rates have changed." Interest rate risk may sound like an odd type of risk, but in fact, it's a common consideration for investors. Be aware that interest rates change on a regular basis, causing some challenging moments. Banks set interest rates, and the primary institution to watch closely is the Federal Reserve (the Fed), which is, in effect, the country's central bank. The Fed raises or lowers its interest rates, actions that, in turn, cause banks to raise or lower their interest rates accordingly. Interest rate changes affect consumers, businesses, and, of course, investors.

Here's a generic introduction to the way fluctuating interest rate risk can affect investors in general: Suppose you buy a long-term, high-quality corporate bond and get a yield of 6 percent. Your money is safe, and your return is locked in at 6 percent. Whew! That's 6 percent. Not bad, huh? But what happens if, after you commit your money, interest rates increase to 8 percent? You lose the opportunity to get that extra 2 percent interest. The only way to get out of your 6 percent bond is to sell it at current market values and use the money to reinvest at the higher rate.

The only problem with this scenario is that the 6 percent bond is likely to drop in value because interest rates rose. Why? Say that the investor is Bob, and the bond yielding 6 percent is a corporate bond issued by Lucin-Muny. According to the bond agreement, Lucin-Muny must pay 6 percent (called the *face rate* or *nominal rate*) during the life of the bond and then, upon maturity, pay the principal. If Bob buys $10,000 of Lucin-Muny bonds on the day they're issued, he gets $600 (of interest) every year for as long as he holds the bonds. If he holds on until maturity, he gets back his $10,000 (the principal). So far so good, right? The plot thickens, however.

Say that Bob decides to sell the bonds long before maturity and that, at the time of the sale, interest rates in the market have risen to 8 percent. Now what? The reality is that no one is going to want his 6 percent bonds if the market is offering bonds at 8 percent. What's Bob to do? He can't change the face rate of 6 percent, and he can't change the fact that only $600 is paid each year for the life of the bonds. What has to change so that current investors get the *equivalent* yield of 8 percent? If you said, "The bonds' value has to go down," bingo! In this example, the bonds' market value needs to drop to $7,500 so that investors buying the bonds get an equivalent yield of 8 percent. (For simplicity's sake, I left out the time it takes for the bonds to mature.) Here's how that figures.

New investors still get $600 annually. However, $600 is equal to 8 percent of $7,500. Therefore, even though investors get the face rate of 6 percent, they get a yield of 8 percent because the actual investment amount is $7,500. In this example, little, if any, financial risk is present, but you see how interest rate risk presents itself. Bob finds out that you can have a good company with a good bond yet still lose $2,500 because of the change in the interest rate. Of course, if Bob doesn't sell, he doesn't realize that loss.

REMEMBER

Historically, rising interest rates have had an adverse effect on stock prices. I outline several reasons why in the following sections. Because the United States is top-heavy in debt, rising interest rates are an obvious risk that threatens both stocks and fixed-income securities (such as bonds).

Hurting a company's financial condition

Rising interest rates have a negative impact on companies that carry a large current debt load or that need to take on more debt, because when interest rates rise, the cost of borrowing money rises, too. Ultimately, the company's profitability and ability to grow are reduced. When a company's profits (or earnings) drop, its stock becomes less desirable, and its stock price falls.

Affecting a company's customers

A company's success comes from selling its products or services. But what happens if increased interest rates negatively impact its customers (specifically, other companies that buy from it)? The financial health of its customers directly affects the company's ability to grow sales and earnings.

For a good example, consider The Home Depot during 2005–2008. The company had soaring sales and earnings during 2005 and into early 2006 as the housing boom hit its high point (record sales, construction, and so on). As the housing bubble popped and the housing and construction industries went into an agonizing decline, the fortunes of The Home Depot followed suit because its success is directly tied to home building, repair, and improvement. By late 2006, The Home Depot's sales were slipping, and earnings were dropping as the housing industry sunk deeper into its depression. This was bad news for stock investors. The Home Depot's stock went from more than $44 in 2005 to $21 by October 2008 (a drop of about 52 percent). Ouch! No "home improvement" there.

The point to keep in mind is that because The Home Depot's fortunes are tied to the housing industry, and this industry is very sensitive and vulnerable to rising interest rates, in an indirect — but significant — way, The Home Depot is also vulnerable. In 2015, The Home Depot was one of the few retail stocks that went up due to the rebounding real estate market.

In the years leading up to 2020, interest rates were historically low. But as inflation became an economic threat during 2021–2022, the Fed began a campaign of raising interest rates. This contributed to the stock market's bear market of 2022, and the rising interest rates also contributed to the inadvertent collapse of several banks such as Silicon Valley Bank and Signature Bank. For investors, it pays to avoid (or minimize exposure to) stocks that are vulnerable to inflation and rising interest rates.

Impacting investors' decision-making

When interest rates rise, investors start to rethink their investment strategies, resulting in one of two outcomes:

» Investors may sell any shares in interest-sensitive stocks that they hold. Interest-sensitive industries include electric utilities, real estate, and the financial sector. Although increased interest rates can hurt these sectors, the reverse is also generally true: Falling interest rates boost the same industries. Keep in mind that interest rate changes affect some industries more than others.

» Investors who favor increased current income (versus waiting for the investment to grow in value to sell for a gain later on) are definitely attracted to investment vehicles that offer a higher yield. Higher interest rates can cause investors to switch from stocks to bonds or bank certificates of deposit (CDs).

Hurting stock prices indirectly

High or rising interest rates can have a negative impact on any investor's total financial picture. What happens when an investor struggles with burdensome debt, such as a second mortgage, credit card debt, or *margin debt* (debt from borrowing against stock in a brokerage account)? They may sell some stock to pay off some of their high-interest debt. Selling stock to service debt is a common practice that, when taken collectively, can hurt stock prices.

As I write this in early 2023, the U.S. economy is struggling as inflation, high debt, and high interest rates take their toll and threaten us with a recession. Expect more risk and volatility for 2023–2024, which is why quality stocks (and exchange-traded funds [ETFs]) are more important than ever. (An *exchange-traded fund* is a fund with a fixed portfolio of stocks or other securities that tracks a particular index but is traded like a stock. By the way, I love ETFs, and I think that every serious investor should consider them; see Chapter 11 for more information.)

Because of the effects of interest rates on stock portfolios, both direct and indirect, successful investors regularly monitor interest rates in both the general economy and in their personal situations. Although stocks have proven to be a superior long-term investment (the longer the term, the better), every investor should maintain a balanced portfolio that includes other investment vehicles. A diversified investor has some money in vehicles that do well when interest rates rise. These vehicles include money-market funds, U.S. savings bonds (series I), and other variable-rate investments whose interest rates rise when market rates rise. These types of investments add a measure of safety from interest rate risk to your stock portfolio. (I discuss diversification in more detail later in this chapter.)

Market risk

People talk about "the market" and how it goes up or down, making it sound like a monolithic entity instead of what it really is — a group of millions of individuals making daily decisions to buy or sell stock. No matter how modern our society and economic system, you can't escape the laws of supply and demand. When masses of people want to buy a particular stock, it becomes in demand, and its price rises. That price rises higher because the supply of stock is limited. Conversely, if no one's interested in buying a stock (and there are folks selling their stock), its price falls. Supply and demand is the nature of market risk. The price of the stock you purchase can rise and fall on the fickle whim of market demand.

Millions of investors buying and selling each minute of every trading day affect the share price of your stock. This fact makes it impossible to judge which way your stock will move tomorrow or next week. This unpredictability and seeming irrationality is why stocks aren't appropriate for short-term financial growth.

Markets are volatile by nature; they go up and down, and investments need time to grow. Market volatility is an increasingly common condition that everyone has to live with (see the later section "Getting the Scoop on Volatility"). Investors should be aware of the fact that stocks in general, especially in today's marketplace, aren't suitable for short-term (one year or less) goals (see Chapters 2 and 3 for more on short-term goals). Despite the fact that companies you're invested in may be fundamentally sound, all stock prices are subject to the gyrations of the marketplace and need time to trend upward.

WARNING

Investing requires diligent work and research before putting your money in quality investments with a long-term perspective. Speculating is attempting to make a relatively quick profit by monitoring the short-term price movements of a particular investment. Investors seek to minimize risk, whereas speculators don't mind risk because it can also magnify profits. Speculating and investing have clear differences, but investors frequently become speculators and ultimately put themselves and their wealth at risk. Don't go there!

Consider the married couple nearing retirement who decided to play with their money in an attempt to make their pending retirement more comfortable. They borrowed a sizable sum by tapping into their home equity to invest in the stock market. (Their home, which they had paid off, had enough equity to qualify for this loan.) What did they do with these funds? You guessed it: They invested in the high-flying stocks of the day, which were high-tech and internet stocks. Within eight months, they lost almost all their money.

WARNING

Understanding market risk is especially important for people who are tempted to put their nest eggs or emergency funds into volatile investments such as growth stocks (or mutual funds that invest in growth stocks or similarly aggressive investment vehicles). *Remember:* You can lose everything.

Inflation risk

Inflation is the artificial expansion of the quantity of money so that too much money is used in exchange for goods and services. To consumers, inflation shows up in the form of higher prices for goods and services. Inflation risk is also referred to as *purchasing power risk*. This term just means that your money doesn't buy as much as it used to. For example, a dollar that bought you a sandwich in 1980 barely bought you a candy bar a few years later. For you, the investor, this risk means that the value of your investment (a stock that doesn't appreciate much, for example) may not keep up with inflation.

Say that you have money in a bank savings account currently earning 4 percent. This account has flexibility — if the market interest rate goes up, the rate you earn in your account goes up. Your account is safe from both financial risk and interest rate risk. But what if inflation is running at 5 percent? At that point you're losing money.

Tax risk

Taxes (such as income tax or capital gains tax) don't affect your stock investment directly, but taxes can obviously affect how much of your money (what portion of your gain) you get to keep. Because the entire point of stock investing is to build wealth, you need to understand that taxes take away a portion of the wealth that you're trying to build. Taxes can be risky because if you make the wrong move with your stocks (selling them at the wrong time, for example), you can end up paying higher taxes than you need to. Because tax laws change so frequently, tax risk is part of the risk-versus-return principle, as well.

It pays to gain knowledge about how taxes can impact your wealth-building program before you make your investment decisions. Chapter 14 covers the impact of taxes in greater detail, and I also touch on the latest tax law changes that may affect you.

Political and governmental risk

If companies were fish, politics and government policies (such as taxes, laws, and regulations) would be the pond. In the same way that fish die in a toxic or polluted pond, politics and government policies can kill companies. Of course, if you own stock in a company exposed to political and governmental risks, you need to be aware of these risks. For some companies, a single new regulation or law is enough to send them into bankruptcy. For other companies, a new law can help them increase sales and profits.

What if you invest in companies or industries that become political targets? You may want to consider selling them (you can always buy them back later) or consider putting in stop-loss orders on the stock (see Chapter 13). For example, tobacco companies were the targets of political firestorms that battered their stock prices. Whether you agree or disagree with the political machinations of today is not the issue. As an investor, you have to ask yourself, "How do politics affect the market value and the current and future prospects of my chosen investment?"

Keep in mind that political risk doesn't just mean in the good ol' U.S. of A.; it can also mean geopolitical risk. Many companies have operations across many countries, and geopolitical events can have a major impact on those companies exposed to risks ranging from governmental risks (such as in Venezuela in 2019) to war and unrest (as in the Middle East) to recessions and economic downturns in friendly countries (such as in Western Europe).

TIP

If international investing interests you, and you see it as a good way to be more diversified (beyond the U.S. stock market), then consider ETFs as a convenient way to do it. (Find out more about international ETFs in Chapter 11.)

Personal risk

Frequently, the risk involved with investing in the stock market isn't directly related to the investment; instead, the risk is associated with the investor's circumstances.

Suppose that investor Ralph puts $15,000 into a portfolio of common stocks. Imagine that the market experiences a drop in prices that week, and Ralph's stocks drop to a market value of $14,000. Because stocks are good for the long term, this type of decrease usually isn't an alarming incident. Odds are that this dip is temporary, especially if Ralph carefully chose high-quality companies. Incidentally, if a portfolio of high-quality stocks *does* experience a temporary drop in price, it can be a great opportunity to get more shares at a good price. (Chapter 13 covers orders you can place with your broker to help you do that.)

Over the long term, Ralph will probably see the value of his investment grow substantially. But what if Ralph experiences financial difficulty and needs quick cash during a period when his stocks are declining? He may have to sell his stock to get some money.

This problem occurs frequently for investors who don't have an emergency fund to handle large, sudden expenses. You never know when your company may lay you off or when your basement may flood, leaving you with a huge repair bill. Car accidents, medical emergencies, and other unforeseen events are part of life's bag of surprises — for anyone.

You probably won't get much comfort from knowing that stock losses are tax-deductible — a loss is a loss (see Chapter 14 for more on taxes). However, you can avoid the kind of loss that results from prematurely having to sell your stocks if you maintain an emergency cash fund. A good place for your emergency cash fund is in either a bank savings account or a money-market fund. Then you aren't forced to prematurely liquidate your stock investments to pay emergency bills. (Chapter 2 provides more guidance on having liquid assets for emergencies.)

Emotional risk

What does emotional risk have to do with stocks? Emotions are important risk considerations because investors are human beings. Logic and discipline are critical factors in investment success, but even the best investor can let emotions take over the reins of money management and cause loss. For stock investing, you're likely to be sidetracked by three main emotions: greed, fear, and love. You need to understand your emotions and what kinds of risk they can expose you to. If you get too attached to a sinking stock, you don't need a stock-investing book — you need a therapist!

Paying the price for greed

In 1998–2000, millions of investors threw caution to the wind and chased highly dubious, risky dot-com stocks. In 2006–2007, investors again chased profits, this time in real estate–bubble related investments (such as home builders and mortgage firms) and got burned in 2008. The dollar signs popped up in their eyes (just like slot machines) when they saw that Easy Street was lined with dot-com stocks that were doubling and tripling in a very short time. Who cares about price-to-earnings (P/E) ratios when you can just buy stock, make a fortune, and get out with millions? (Of course, *you* care about making money with stocks, so you can flip to Chapter 6 to find out more about P/E ratios.)

Unfortunately, the lure of the easy buck can easily turn healthy attitudes about growing wealth into unhealthy greed that blinds investors and discards common sense. Avoid the temptation to invest for short-term gains in dubious hot stocks instead of doing your homework and buying stocks of solid companies with strong fundamentals and a long-term focus, as I explain in Part 2.

Recognizing the role of fear

Greed can be a problem, but fear is the other extreme. People who are fearful of loss frequently avoid suitable investments and end up settling for a low rate of return. If you have to succumb to one of these emotions, at least fear exposes you to less loss.

Also, keep in mind that fear is frequently a symptom of lack of knowledge about what's going on. If you see your stocks falling and don't understand why, fear will take over, and you may act irrationally. When stock investors are affected by fear, they tend to sell their stocks and head for the exits and the lifeboats. When an investor sees their stock go down 20 percent, what goes through their head? Experienced, knowledgeable investors realize that no bull market goes straight up. Even the strongest bull goes up in a zigzag fashion. Conversely, even bear markets don't go straight down; they zigzag down. Out of fear, inexperienced investors sell good stocks when they see them go down temporarily (the *correction*), whereas experienced investors see that temporary downward move as a good buying opportunity to add to their positions.

Looking for love in all the wrong places

Stocks are dispassionate, inanimate vehicles, but people can look for love in the strangest places. Emotional risk occurs when investors fall in love with a stock and refuse to sell it, even when the stock is plummeting and shows all the symptoms of getting worse. Emotional risk also occurs when investors are drawn to bad investment choices just because they sound good, are popular, or are pushed by family or friends. Love and attachment are great in relationships with people but can be horrible with investments. To deal with this emotion, investors have to deploy techniques that take the emotion out. For example, you can use brokerage orders (such as trailing stops and limit orders; see Chapter 13), which can automatically trigger buy and sell transactions and leave out some of the agonizing. Hey, disciplined investing may just become your new passion!

Getting the Scoop on Volatility

How often have you heard a financial reporter on TV say, "Well, it looks like a volatile day as the markets plunge 700 points. . . ." Oh, dear, pass me the antacid! Volatility has garnered a bad reputation because roller coasters and weak stomachs don't mix — especially when your financial future seems to be acting like a kite in a tornado.

People may think of volatility as "risk on steroids," but you need to understand what volatility actually is. Technically, it isn't really good or bad (although it's usually associated with bad movements in the marketplace). *Volatility* is the movement of an asset (or the entire market) very quickly down (or up) in price due to large selling (or buying) in a very short period of time.

Volatility tends to be more associated with the negative because of crowd psychology. People are more likely to act quickly (sell!) because of fear than because of other motivators (such as greed; see the earlier section "Emotional risk" for more info). More people are apt to run for the exits than they are to run to the entrance, so to speak.

Not all stocks are equal with regard to volatility. Some can be very volatile, whereas others can be quite stable. A good way to determine a stock's volatility is to look at the beta of the stock. *Beta* is a statistical measure that attempts to give the investor a clue as to how volatile a stock may be. It's determined by comparing the potential volatility of a particular stock to the market in general. The market (as represented by, say, the S&P 500) is assigned a beta of 1. Any stock with a beta greater than 1 is considered more volatile than the general stock market, whereas any stock with a beta of less than 1 is considered less volatile. If a stock has a beta of 1.5, for example, it's considered 50 percent more volatile than the general market. Meanwhile, a stock with a beta of 0.85 is considered 15 percent less volatile than the general stock market. In other words, this stock would decline 8.5 percent if the market were to decline 10 percent.

TIP

Therefore, if you don't want to keep gulping down more antacid, consider stocks that have a beta of less than 1. You can easily find the beta in the stock report pages that are usually provided by major financial websites such as Yahoo! Finance (https://finance.yahoo.com) and MarketWatch (www.marketwatch.com).

WHY MORE VOLATILITY?

People will always gasp at the occasional big up or down day, but volatility is more prevalent overall today than it was a few decades ago. Why is that? There are several contributing factors:

- **Today's investor has the advantages of cheaper commissions and faster technology.** Years ago, if an investor wanted to sell, they had to call their broker — usually during business hours. On top of that, the commission was usually $30 or higher. That discouraged a lot of rapid-fire trading. Today, trading is not only cheaper (with web-based discount brokers), but anyone can do it from home with a few clicks of a mouse on a website literally 24 hours a day, 7 days a week.

- **Large organizations — ranging from financial institutions to government-sponsored entities such as sovereign wealth funds — can make large trades of huge amounts of money either nationally or globally within split seconds.** The rapid movement of large amounts of money both in and out of a stock or an entire market means that volatility is high and likely to be with us for a long time to come.

- **The world is now more of a global marketplace, and our markets react more to international events than in the past.** With new technology and the internet, news travels farther and faster than ever before.

Minimizing Your Risk

Now, before you go crazy thinking that stock investing carries so much risk that you may as well not get out of bed, take a breath. Minimizing your risk in stock investing is easier than you think. Although wealth building through the stock market doesn't take place without some amount of risk, you can practice the following tips to maximize your profits and still keep your money secure.

Gaining knowledge

Some people spend more time analyzing a restaurant menu to choose a $20 entrée than analyzing where to put their next $5,000. Lack of knowledge constitutes the greatest risk for new investors, so diminishing that risk starts with gaining knowledge.

The more familiar you are with the stock market — how it works, factors that affect stock value, and so on — the better you can navigate around its pitfalls and maximize your profits. The same knowledge that enables you to grow your wealth also enables you to minimize your risk. Before you put your money anywhere, you want to know as much as you can. This book is a great place to start — check out Chapter 5 for a rundown of the kinds of information you want to know before you buy stocks, as well as the resources that can give you the information you need to invest successfully.

Staying out until you get a little practice

If you don't understand stocks, don't invest! Yeah, I know this book is about stock investing, and I think that some measure of stock investing is a good idea for most people. But that doesn't mean you should be 100 percent invested 100 percent of the time. If you don't understand a particular stock (or don't understand stocks, period), stay away until you do. Instead, give yourself an imaginary sum of money, such as $100,000, give yourself reasons to invest, and just make believe (a practice called *simulated stock investing*). Pick a few stocks that you think will increase in value, track them for a while, and see how they perform. Begin to understand how the price of a stock goes up and down, and watch what happens to the stocks you choose when various events take place. As you find out more about stock investing, you get better at picking individual stocks, without risking — or losing — any money during your learning period.

TIP

A good place to do your imaginary investing is on websites such as HowTheMarketWorks.com (www.howthemarketworks.com). You can design a stock portfolio and track its performance with thousands of other investors to see how well you do.

Putting your financial house in order

Advice on what to do before you invest could be a whole book all by itself. The bottom line is that you want to make sure that you are, first and foremost, financially secure before you take the plunge into the stock market. If you're not sure about your financial security, look over your situation with a financial planner.

Before you buy your first stock, here are a few things you can do to get your finances in order:

>> **Have a cushion of money.** Set aside three to six months' worth of your gross living expenses somewhere safe, such as in a bank account or Treasury money-market fund, in case you suddenly need cash for an emergency (see Chapter 2 for details).

>> **Reduce your debt.** Overindulging in debt was the worst personal economic problem for many Americans in the late 1990s, and this practice has continued in recent years. Ideally, you should strive to have zero credit card debt; interest rates on credit cards are very high, so getting to zero as soon as possible is a sure wealth-building strategy!

>> **Make sure that your job is as secure as you can make it.** Are you keeping your skills up to date? Is the company you work for strong and growing? Is the industry that you work in strong and growing?

>> **Make sure that you have adequate insurance.** You need enough insurance to cover your needs and those of your family in case of illness, death, disability, and so on.

Diversifying your investments

Diversification is a strategy for reducing risk by spreading your money across different investments. It's a fancy way of saying, "Don't put all your eggs in one basket." But how do you go about divvying up your money and distributing it among different investments?

The easiest way to understand proper diversification may be to look at what you *shouldn't* do:

>> **Don't put all your money in one stock.** Sure, if you choose wisely and select a hot stock, you may make a bundle, but the odds are tremendously against you. Unless you're a real expert on a particular company, it's a good idea to have small portions of your money in several different stocks. As a general rule, the money you tie up in a single stock should be money you can do without.

>> **Don't put all your money in one industry.** I know people who own several stocks, but the stocks are all in the same industry. Again, if you're an expert in that particular industry, it can work out. But just understand that you're not properly diversified. If a problem hits an entire industry, you may get hurt.

>> **Don't put all your money in one type of investment.** Stocks may be a great investment, but you need to have money elsewhere. Bonds, bank accounts, Treasury securities, real estate, and precious metals are perennial alternatives to complement your stock portfolio. Some of these alternatives can be found in mutual funds or ETFs.

Okay, now that you know what you *shouldn't* do, what *should* you do? Until you become more knowledgeable, follow this advice:

>> **Keep only 5 percent to 10 percent (or less) of your investment money in a single stock.** Because you want adequate diversification, you don't want overexposure to a single stock. Aggressive investors can certainly go for 10 percent or even higher, but conservative investors are better off at 5 percent or less.

>> **Invest in four or five (and no more than ten) different stocks that are in different industries.** Which industries? Choose industries that offer products and services that have shown strong, growing demand. To make this decision, use your common sense (which isn't as common as it used to be). Think about the industries that people need no matter what happens in the general economy, such as food, energy, and other consumer necessities. (See Chapter 12 for more information about analyzing sectors and industries.)

Weighing Risk against Return

How much risk is appropriate for you, and how do you handle it? Before you try to figure out what risks accompany your investment choices, analyze yourself. Here are some points to keep in mind when weighing risk versus return in your situation:

>> **Your financial goal:** In five minutes with a financial calculator, you can easily see how much money you're going to need to become financially independent (presuming financial independence is your goal). Say that you need $500,000 in ten years for a worry-free retirement and that your financial assets (such as stocks, bonds, and so on) are currently worth $400,000. In this scenario, your assets need to grow by only 2.25 percent to hit your target. Getting investments that grow by 2.25 percent safely is easy to do because that's a relatively low rate of return.

The important point is that you don't have to knock yourself out trying to double your money with risky, high-flying investments; some run-of-the-mill bank investments will do just fine. All too often, investors take on more risk than is necessary. Figure out what your financial goal is so that you know what kind of return you realistically need. (Turn to Chapters 2 and 3 for details on determining your financial goals.)

>> **Your investor profile:** Are you nearing retirement, or are you fresh out of college? Your life situation matters when it comes to looking at risk versus return.

If you're just beginning your working years, you can certainly tolerate greater risk than someone facing retirement. Even if you lose big time, you still have a long time to recoup your money and get back on track.

However, if you're within five years of retirement, risky or aggressive investments can do much more harm than good. If you lose money, you don't have as much time to recoup your investment, and odds are that you'll need the investment money (and its income-generating capacity) to cover your living expenses after you're no longer employed.

>> **Asset allocation:** I never tell retirees to put a large portion of their retirement money into a high-tech stock or other volatile investment. But if they still want to speculate, I don't see a problem as long as they limit such investments to 5 percent of their total assets. As long as the bulk of their money is safe and sound in secure investments (such as U.S. Treasury bonds), I know I can sleep well (knowing that *they* can sleep well!).

REMEMBER

Asset allocation beckons back to diversification, which I discuss earlier in this chapter. For people in their 20s and 30s, having 75 percent of their money in a diversified portfolio of growth stocks (such as mid-cap and small-cap stocks; see Chapter 1) is acceptable. For people in their 60s and 70s, it's not acceptable; they may, instead, consider investing no more than 20 percent of their money in stocks (mid caps and large caps are preferable). Check with your financial advisor to find the right mix for your particular situation.

2

Doing Some Digging Before You Buy Stocks

IN THIS CHAPTER

» **Using stock exchanges to get investment information**

» **Applying accounting and economic know-how to your investments**

» **Keeping abreast of financial news**

» **Deciphering stock tables**

» **Understanding dividend dates**

» **Recognizing good (and bad) investing advice**

Chapter **5**

Gathering Information on Investments

Knowledge and information are two critical success factors in stock investing. (Isn't that true about most things in life?) People who plunge headlong into stocks without sufficient knowledge of the stock market in general and current information in particular quickly learn the lesson of the eager diver who didn't find out ahead of time that the pool was only an inch deep (ouch!). In their haste to avoid missing so-called golden investment opportunities, investors too often end up losing money.

REMEMBER

Opportunities to *make* money in the stock market will always be there, no matter how well or how poorly the economy and the market are performing in general. There's no such thing as a single (and fleeting) magical moment, so don't feel that if you let an opportunity pass you by, you'll always regret that you missed your one big chance.

For the best approach to stock investing, build your knowledge and find quality information first so you can make your fortunes more assuredly. Before you buy, you need to know that the company you're investing in is

>> Financially sound and growing

>> Offering products and/or services that are in demand by consumers

>> In a strong and growing industry (and general economy)

Where do you start, and what kind of information do you want to acquire? Keep reading.

Looking to Stock Exchanges for Answers

Before you invest in stocks, you need to be completely familiar with the basics of stock investing. At its most fundamental, stock investing is about using your money to buy a piece of a company that will give you value in the form of appreciation or income (or both). Fortunately, many resources are available to help you find out about stock investing. Some of my favorite places are the stock exchanges themselves.

Stock exchanges are organized marketplaces for the buying and selling of stocks (and other securities). The New York Stock Exchange (NYSE; also referred to as the *Big Board*), the premier stock exchange, provides a framework for stock buyers and sellers to make their transactions. The NYSE makes money not only from a cut of every transaction but also from fees (such as listing fees) charged to companies and brokers that are members of its exchanges. In 2007, the NYSE merged with Euronext, a major European exchange, but no material differences exist for stock investors. In 2008, the American Stock Exchange (Amex) was taken over by (and completely merged into) the NYSE. The new name is NYSE American.

The main exchanges for most stock investors are the NYSE (www.nyse.com) and Nasdaq (www.nasdaq.com). Technically, Nasdaq isn't an exchange, but it's a formal market that effectively acts as an exchange. Because the NYSE and Nasdaq benefit from the increased popularity of stock investing and continued demand for stocks, they offer a wealth of free (or low-cost) resources and information for stock investors. Go to their websites to find useful resources, such as the following:

>> Tutorials on how to invest in stocks, common investment strategies, and so on

>> Glossaries and free information to help you understand the language, practice, and purpose of stock investing

>> A wealth of news, press releases, financial data, and other information about companies listed on the exchange or market, usually accessed through an on-site search engine

>> Industry analysis and news

>> Stock quotes and other market information related to the daily market movements of stocks, including data such as volume, new highs, new lows, and so on

>> Free tracking of your stock selections (you can input a sample portfolio or the stocks you're following to see how well you're doing)

TIP

What each exchange/market offers keeps changing and is often updated, so explore their websites periodically.

Grasping the Basics of Accounting and Economics

Stocks represent ownership in companies. Before you buy individual stocks, you want to understand the companies whose stock you're considering and find out about their operations. It may sound like a daunting task, but you'll digest the point more easily when you realize that companies work very similarly to the way you work. They make decisions on a daily basis just as you do.

Think about how you grow and prosper as an individual or as a family, and you see the same issues with businesses and how they grow and prosper. Low earnings and high debt are examples of financial difficulties that affect both people and companies. You can better understand companies' finances by taking the time to pick up some information in two basic disciplines: accounting and economics. These two disciplines, which I discuss in the following sections, play a significant role in understanding the performance of a firm's stock.

Accounting for taste and a whole lot more

Accounting. Ugh! But face it: Accounting is the language of business, and believe it or not, you're already familiar with the most important accounting concepts! Just look at the following three essential principles:

» **Assets minus liabilities equals net worth.** In other words, take what you own (your *assets*), subtract what you owe (your *liabilities*), and the rest is yours (your *net worth*)! Your own personal finances work the same way as Microsoft's (except yours have fewer zeros at the end). See Chapter 2 to figure out how to calculate your own net worth.

   A company's *balance sheet* shows you its net worth at a specific point in time (such as December 31). The net worth of a company is the bottom line of its asset and liability picture, and it tells you whether the company is *solvent* (has the ability to pay its debts without going out of business). The net worth of a successful company grows regularly. To see whether your company is successful, compare its net worth with the net worth from the same point a year earlier. A firm that has a $4 million net worth on December 31, 2018, and a $5 million net worth on December 31, 2019, is doing well; its net worth has gone up 25 percent ($1 million) in one year.

» **Income minus expenses equals net income.** In other words, take what you make (your *income*), subtract what you spend (your *expenses*), and the remainder is your gain (your *net income,* also known as *net profit* or *net earnings*).

   A company's profitability is the whole point of investing in its stock. As it profits, the business becomes more valuable, and in turn, its stock price becomes more valuable. To discover a firm's net income, look at its income statement. Try to determine whether the company uses its gains wisely, either by reinvesting them for continued growth or by paying down debt.

» **Do a comparative financial analysis.** That's a mouthful, but it's just a fancy way of saying how a company is doing now compared with something else (like a prior period or a similar company).

If you know that the company you're looking at had a net income of $50,000 for the year, you may ask, "Is that good or bad?" Obviously, making a net profit is good, but you also need to know whether it's good compared to something else. If the company had a net profit of $40,000 the year before, you know that the company's profitability is improving. But if a similar company had a net profit of $100,000 the year before and in the current year it's making $50,000, then you may want to either avoid the company making the lesser profit or see what (if anything) went wrong with the company making less.

Accounting can be this simple. If you understand these three basic points, you're ahead of the curve (in stock investing as well as in your personal finances). For more information on how to use a company's financial statements to pick good stocks, turn to Chapters 6 and 7.

Understanding how economics affects stocks

Economics. Double ugh! No, you aren't required to understand "the inelasticity of demand aggregates" (thank heavens!) or "marginal utility" (say what?). But a working knowledge of basic economics is crucial — and I mean *crucial* — to your success and proficiency as a stock investor. The stock market and the economy are joined at the hip. The good (or bad) things that happen to one have a direct effect on the other. The following sections give you the lowdown.

Getting the hang of the basic concepts

REMEMBER

Alas, many investors get lost on basic economic concepts (as do some so-called experts you see on TV). I owe my personal investing success to my status as a student of economics. Understanding basic economics helps me (and will help you) filter the financial news to separate relevant information from the irrelevant in order to make better investment decisions. Be aware of these important economic concepts:

>> **Supply and demand:** How can anyone possibly think about economics without thinking of the ageless concept of supply and demand? *Supply and demand* can be simply stated as the relationship between what's available (the *supply*) and what

people want and are willing to pay for (the *demand*). This equation is the main engine of economic activity and is extremely important for your stock investing analysis and decision-making process. I mean, do you really want to buy stock in a company that makes elephant-foot umbrella stands if you find out that the company has an oversupply and nobody wants to buy them anyway?

>> **Cause and effect:** If you pick up a prominent news report and read, "Companies in the table industry are expecting plummeting sales," do you rush out and invest in companies that sell chairs or manufacture tablecloths? Considering cause and effect is an exercise in logical thinking, and believe you me, logic is a major component of sound economic thought.

TIP

When you read business news, play it out in your mind. What good (or bad) can logically be expected given a certain event or situation? If you're looking for an effect ("I want a stock price that keeps increasing"), you also want to understand the cause.

Here are some typical events that can cause a stock's price to rise:

- **Positive news reports about a company:** The news may report that the company is enjoying success with increased sales or a new product.

- **Positive news reports about a company's industry:** The media may be highlighting that the industry is poised to do well.

- **Positive news reports about a company's customers:** Maybe your company is in industry A, but its customers are in industry B. If you see good news about industry B, that may be good news for your stock.

- **Negative news reports about a company's competitors:** If the competitors are in trouble, their customers may seek alternatives to buy from, including your company.

>> **Economic effects from government actions:** Political and governmental actions have economic consequences. As a matter of fact, *nothing* has a greater effect on investing and economics than government. Government actions usually

manifest themselves as taxes, laws, or regulations. They also can take on a more ominous appearance, such as war or the threat of war. Government can willfully (or even accidentally) cause a company to go bankrupt, disrupt an entire industry, or even cause a depression. Government controls the money supply, credit, and all public securities markets.

Gaining insight from past mistakes

History is littered with the damage done to the investing public because they didn't understand or didn't heed the greater issues that faced their investments.

The famous stock market crash of 1929 didn't "just happen" as if it were a surprise meteor bombardment hitting Wall Street in the dead of night. The stock market was a dangerous bubble that was years in the making due to the Federal Reserve's overproduction of the money supply coupled with America's speculative excess with debt and spending. Prudent investors saw this and started to pull back or limit their exposure. Famed speculators such as Jesse Livermore watched this and he shorted the stock and made a staggering $100 million gain (the equivalent of more than $1 billion in today's dollars).

In crisis after crisis, investors who ignore economics have gotten whacked in the bear markets that always arrive at the end of rampant speculation and speculative excess. The bear market of 1973–1975 was brutal (a drop of about 40 percent), but astute investors (such as Warren Buffett) used the downturn as a spectacular buying opportunity. Similar machinations occurred for investors during the 2008 crisis, the 2020 pandemic, and the 2022 bear market. Again, understanding basic economics has helped investors either avoid or minimize losses or has helped them get profitably set up for the subsequent bull market.

When the stock market bubble popped during 2000–2002, it was soon replaced with the housing bubble, which popped during 2005–2006. And February 2020 witnessed a major correction (the Dow Jones Industrials, for example, fell over 11 percent during the five trading days ending February 28, 2020) over fears due to the coronavirus originating in China and causing a worldwide panic.

Of course, you should always be happy to earn 25 percent per year with your investments, but such a return can't be sustained and encourages speculation. This artificial stimulation by the Fed resulted in the following:

>> **More and more people depleted their savings.** After all, why settle for less than 1 percent in the bank when you can get so much more in the stock market?

>> **More and more people bought on credit (such as auto loans, brokerage margin loans, and so on).** If the economy is booming, why not buy now and pay later? Consumer credit hit record highs.

>> **More and more people borrowed against their homes.** Why not borrow and get rich now? "I can pay off my debt later" was at the forefront of these folks' minds at the time.

>> **More and more companies sold more goods as consumers took more vacations and bought SUVs, electronics, and so on.** Companies then borrowed to finance expansion, open new stores, and so on.

>> **More and more companies went public and offered stock.** This strategy enabled them to take advantage of the increase in money that was flowing to the markets from banks and other financial institutions.

In the end, spending started to slow down because consumers and businesses became too indebted. This slowdown, in turn, caused the sales of goods and services to taper off. Companies were left with too much overhead, capacity, and debt because they had expanded too eagerly. At this point, businesses were caught in a financial bind. Too much debt and too many expenses in a slowing economy mean one thing: Profits shrink or disappear. To stay in business, companies had to do the logical thing — cut expenses. What's usually the biggest expense for companies? People! Many companies started laying off employees. As a result, consumer spending dropped further because more people either were laid off or had second thoughts about their own job security.

Because people had little in the way of savings and too much in the way of debt, they had to sell their stocks to pay their bills. This trend was a major reason that stocks started to fall in 2000. Earnings started to drop because of shrinking sales from a sputtering economy. As earnings fell, stock prices also fell.

With some hiccups along the way, the stock market has solidly zigzagged upward since the early 2000s, and the Dow Jones breached the 29,000 level in early 2020, but investors should be just as wary when the market is at nosebleed levels as they are when bear markets hit because market highs tend to be followed by the next bear market or downward move. In February 2020, stock markets did correct painfully (a fall of 10 percent or more is a *correction*; a fall of 20 percent or more is a *bear market*), and they offered a buying opportunity for value-oriented investors.

The lessons from the 1990s and the 2000–2022 time frame are important ones for investors today:

>> Stocks are not a replacement for savings accounts. Always have some money in the bank.

>> Stocks should never occupy 100 percent of your investment funds.

>> When anyone (including an expert) tells you that the economy will keep growing indefinitely, be skeptical and read diverse sources of information.

>> If stocks do well in your portfolio, consider protecting your stocks (both your original investment and any gains) with stop-loss orders. (See Chapter 13 for more on these strategies.)

>> Keep debt and expenses to a minimum.

>> If the economy is booming, a decline is sure to follow as the ebb and flow of the economy's business cycle continues.

KNOW THYSELF BEFORE YOU INVEST IN STOCKS

If you're reading this book, you're probably doing so because you want to become a successful investor. Granted, to be a successful investor, you have to select great stocks, but having a realistic understanding of your own financial situation and goals is equally important.

(continued)

(continued)

I recall one investor who lost $10,000 in a speculative stock. The loss wasn't that bad because he had most of his money safely tucked away elsewhere. He also understood that his overall financial situation was secure and that the money he lost was "play money" — the loss wouldn't have a drastic effect on his life. But many investors often lose even more money, and the loss does have a major, negative effect on their lives. You may not be like the investor who can afford to lose $10,000.

Take time to understand yourself, your own financial picture, and your personal investment goals before you decide to buy stocks. (See Chapter 2 for guidance.)

Staying on Top of Financial News

Reading the financial news can help you decide where or where not to invest. Many newspapers, magazines, and websites offer great coverage of the financial world. Obviously, the more informed you are, the better, but you don't have to read everything that's written. The information explosion in recent years has gone beyond overload, and you can easily spend so much time reading that you have little time left for investing. In the following sections, I describe the types of information you need to get from the financial news.

TIP

Check out the following resources to get started:

>> The most obvious publications of interest to stock investors are *The Wall Street Journal* (www.wsj.com) and *Investor's Business Daily* (www.investors.com). These excellent publications report the news and stock data as of the prior trading day.

>> Some of the more obvious websites are MarketWatch (www.marketwatch.com), Yahoo! Finance (https://finance.yahoo.com), Bloomberg (www.bloomberg.com), ZeroHedge (www.zerohedge.com), and Investing.com (www.investing.com). These websites can actually give you news and stock data within minutes after an event occurs.

>> Don't forget the exchanges' websites (see the earlier section "Looking to Stock Exchanges for Answers").

Figuring out what a company is up to

Before you invest, you need to know what's going on with the company. When you read about the company, either from the firm's literature (its annual report, for example) or from media sources, be sure to get answers to some pertinent questions:

>> **Is the company making more net income than it did last year?** You want to invest in a company that's growing.

>> **Are the company's sales greater than they were the year before?** Keep in mind that you won't make money if the company isn't making money.

>> **Is the company issuing press releases on new products, services, inventions, or business deals?** All these achievements indicate a strong, vital company.

Knowing how the company is doing, no matter what's happening with the general economy, is obviously important. (To better understand how companies tick, see Chapters 6 and 7.)

Discovering what's new with an industry

As you consider investing in a stock, make a point of knowing what's going on in that company's industry. If the industry is doing well, your stock is likely to do well, too. But then again, the reverse is also true.

Yes, I've seen investors pick successful stocks in a failing industry, but those cases are exceptional. By and large, it's easier to succeed with a stock when the entire industry is doing well. As you're watching the news, reading the financial pages, or perusing financial websites, check out the industry to ensure that it's strong and dynamic. (See Chapter 12 for information on analyzing sectors and megatrends.)

Knowing what's happening with the economy

No matter how well or how poorly the overall economy is performing, you want to stay informed about its general progress.

It's easier for the value of a stock to keep going up when the economy is stable or growing. The reverse is also true: If the economy is contracting or declining, the stock has a tougher time keeping its value. Some basic items to keep tabs on include the following:

>> **Gross domestic product (GDP):** The GDP is roughly the total value of output for a particular nation, measured in the dollar amount of goods and services. It's reported quarterly, and a rising GDP bodes well for your stock. When the GDP is rising 3 percent or more on an annual basis, that's solid growth. If it rises but is less than 3 percent, that's generally considered less-than-stellar (or mediocre). A GDP under zero (a negative number) means that the economy is shrinking (heading into recession).

>> **The Leading Economic Index (LEI):** The LEI is a snapshot of a set of economic statistics covering activity that precedes what's happening in the economy. Each statistic helps you understand the economy in much the same way that barometers (and windows!) help you understand what's happening with the weather. Economists don't just look at an individual statistic; they look at a set of statistics to get a more complete picture of what's happening with the economy.

Seeing what public officials are doing

Being informed about what public officials are doing is vital to your success as a stock investor. Because federal, state, and local governments pass literally thousands of laws, rules, and regulations every year, monitoring the political landscape is critical to your success. The news media report what the president and Congress are doing, so always ask yourself, "How does a new law, tax, or regulation affect my stock investment?"

TIP

You can find laws being proposed or enacted by the federal government through Congress's search page (www.congress.gov). Also, some great organizations — such as the National Taxpayers Union (www.ntu.org) and the Tax Foundation (https://taxfoundation.org) — inform the public about tax laws and their impact.

Checking for trends in society, culture, and entertainment

As odd as it sounds, trends in society, popular culture, and entertainment affect your investments, directly or indirectly. For example, when you see a headline such as "Millennials Outnumber Baby Boomers," you should find out what their buying habits are, what products and services they favor, and so on. Understanding the basics of demographic shifts can give you some important insights that can help you make wiser long-term choices in your stock portfolio. With that particular headline, you know that companies that are well positioned to cater to that growing market's wants and needs will do well — meaning a successful stock pick for you.

Keep your eyes open to emerging trends in society at large by reading and viewing the media that cover such matters (*Time* magazine, CNN, and so on). What trends are evident now? Can you anticipate the wants and needs of tomorrow's society? Being alert, staying a step ahead of the public, and choosing stocks appropriately gives you a profitable edge over other investors. If you own stock in a solid company with growing sales and earnings, other investors eventually notice. As more investors buy up your company's stock, you're rewarded as the stock price increases.

Reading (and Understanding) Stock Tables

The stock tables in major business publications such as *The Wall Street Journal* and *Investor's Business Daily* are loaded with information that can help you become a savvy investor — if you know how to interpret them. You need the information in the stock tables for more than selecting promising investment opportunities. You also need to consult the tables after you invest to monitor how your stocks are doing.

Looking at the stock tables without knowing what you're looking for or why you're looking is the equivalent of reading *War and Peace* backward through a kaleidoscope — nothing makes sense. But I can help you make sense of it all (well, at least the stock tables!). Table 5-1 shows a sample stock table. Each item gives you some clues about the current state of affairs for that particular company. The sections that follow describe each column to help you understand what you're looking at.

TABLE 5-1   A Sample Stock Table

52-Wk High	52-Wk Low	Name (Symbol)	Div	Vol	Yld	P/E	Day Last	Net Chg
21.50	8.00	SkyHigh Corp (SHC)		3,143		76	21.25	+.25
47.00	31.75	LowDown Inc (LDI)	2.35	2,735	5.9	18	41.00	–.50
25.00	21.00	ValueNow Inc (VNI)	1.00	1,894	4.5	12	22.00	+.10
83.00	33.00	DoinBadly Corp (DBC)		7,601			33.50	–.75

REMEMBER

Every newspaper's financial tables are a little different, but they give you basically the same information. Updated daily, these tables aren't the place to start your search for a good stock; they're usually where your search ends. The stock tables are the place to look when you own a stock or know what you want to buy, and you're just checking to see the most recent price.

52-week high

The column in Table 6-1 labeled "52-Wk High" gives you the highest price that particular stock has reached in the most recent 52-week period. Knowing this price lets you gauge where the stock is now versus where it has been recently. SkyHighCorp's (SHC) stock has been as high as $21.50, whereas its last (most recent) price is $21.25, the number listed in the "Day Last" column. (Flip to the later section "Day last" for more on understanding this information.) SkyHighCorp's stock is trading very high right now because it's hovering right near its overall 52-week high figure.

Now, take a look at DoinBadlyCorp's (DBC) stock price. It seems to have tumbled big time. Its stock price has had a high in the past 52 weeks of $83, but it's currently trading at $33.50. Something just doesn't seem right here. During the past 52 weeks,

DBC's stock price has fallen dramatically. If you're thinking about investing in DBC, find out why the stock price has fallen. If the company is strong, it may be a good opportunity to buy stock at a lower price. If the company is having tough times, avoid it. In any case, research the firm and find out why its stock has declined. (Chapters 6 and 7 provide the basics of researching companies.)

52-week low

The column labeled "52-Wk Low" gives you the lowest price that particular stock reached in the most recent 52-week period. Again, this information is crucial to your ability to analyze stock over a period of time. Look at DBC in Table 6-1, and you can see that its current trading price of $33.50 in the "Day Last" column is close to its 52-week low of $33.

REMEMBER

Keep in mind that the high and low prices just give you a range of how far that particular stock's price has moved within the past 52 weeks. They can alert you that a stock has problems or tell you that a stock's price has fallen enough to make it a bargain. Simply reading the "52-Wk High" and "52-Wk Low" columns isn't enough to determine which of those two scenarios is happening. They basically tell you to get more information before you commit your money.

Name and symbol

The "Name (Symbol)" column is the simplest in Table 6-1. It tells you the company name (usually abbreviated) and the stock symbol assigned to the company.

TIP

When you have your eye on a stock for potential purchase, get familiar with its symbol. Knowing the symbol makes it easier for you to find your stock in the financial tables, which lists stocks in alphabetical order by the company's name (or symbol depending on the source). Stock symbols are the language of stock investing, and you need to use them in all stock communications, from getting a stock quote at your broker's office to buying stock over the internet.

Dividend

Dividends (shown under the "Div" column in Table 6-1) are basically payments to owners (stockholders). If a company pays a dividend, it's shown in the dividend column. The amount you see is the annual dividend quoted for one share of that stock. If you look at LowDownInc (LDI) in Table 6-1, you can see that you get $2.35 as an annual dividend for each share of stock that you own. Companies usually pay the dividend in quarterly amounts. If I own 100 shares of LDI, the company pays me a quarterly dividend of $58.75 ($235 total per year). A healthy company strives to maintain or upgrade the dividend for stockholders from year to year. (I discuss additional dividend details later in this chapter.)

The dividend is very important to investors seeking income from their stock investments. For more about investing for income, see Chapter 10. Investors buy stocks in companies that don't pay dividends primarily for growth. For more information on growth stocks, see Chapter 9.

Volume

Normally, when you hear the word *volume* on the news, it refers to how much stock is bought and sold for the entire market: "Well, stocks were very active today. Trading volume at the NYSE hit 2 billion shares." Volume is certainly important to watch because the stocks that you're investing in are somewhere in that activity. For the "Vol" column in Table 6-1, though, the volume refers to the individual stock.

Volume tells you how many shares of that particular stock were traded that day. If only 100 shares are traded in a day, then the trading volume is 100. SHC had 3,143 shares change hands on the trading day represented in Table 6-1. Is that good or bad? Neither, really. Usually the business news media mention volume for a particular stock only when it's unusually large. If a stock normally has volume in the 5,000 to 10,000 range, and all of a sudden it has a trading volume of 87,000, it's time to sit up and take notice.

REMEMBER

Keep in mind that a low trading volume for one stock may be a high trading volume for another stock. You can't necessarily compare one stock's volume against that of any other company. The large-cap stocks like IBM or Microsoft typically have trading volumes in the millions of shares almost every day, whereas less-active, smaller stocks may have average trading volumes in far, far smaller numbers.

The main point to remember is that trading volume that is far in excess of that stock's normal range is a sign that something is going on with that company. It may be negative or positive, but something newsworthy is happening with that company. If the news is positive, the increased volume is a result of more people buying the stock. If the news is negative, the increased volume is probably a result of more people selling the stock. What are typical events that cause increased trading volume? Some positive reasons include the following:

>> **Good earnings reports:** The company announces good (or better-than-expected) earnings.

>> **A new business deal:** The firm announces a favorable business deal, such as a joint venture, or lands a big client.

>> **A new product or service:** The company's research and development (R&D) department creates a potentially profitable new product.

>> **Indirect benefits:** The business may benefit from a new development in the economy or from a new law passed by Congress.

Some negative reasons for an unusually large fluctuation in trading volume for a particular stock include the following:

>> **Bad earnings reports:** Profit is the lifeblood of a company. When a company's profits fall or disappear, you see more volume.

>> **Governmental problems:** The stock is being targeted by government action, such as a lawsuit or a Securities and Exchange Commission (SEC) probe.

>> **Liability issues:** The media report that the company has a defective product or similar problem.

>> **Financial problems:** Independent analysts report that the company's financial health is deteriorating.

REMEMBER

Check out what's happening when you hear about heavier-than-usual volume (especially if you already own the stock).

Yield

In general, yield is a return on the money you invest. However, in the stock tables, *yield* ("Yld" in Table 6-1) is a reference to what percentage that particular dividend is of the stock price. Yield is most important to *income investors* (people who invest in stocks as a means of generating regular income; see Chapter 10). Yield is calculated by dividing the annual dividend by the current stock price. In Table 6-1, you can see that the yield du jour of Value-NowInc (VNI) is 4.5 percent (a dividend of $1 divided by the company's stock price of $22). Notice that many companies report no yield; because they have no dividends, their yield is zero.

REMEMBER

Keep in mind that the yield reported on the financial sites changes daily as the stock price changes. Yield is always reported as if you're buying the stock that day. If you buy VNI on the day represented in Table 6-1, your yield is 4.5 percent. But what if VNI's stock price rises to $30 the following day? Investors who buy stock at $30 per share obtain a yield of just 3.3 percent (the dividend of $1 divided by the new stock price, $30). Of course, because you bought the stock at $22, you essentially locked in the prior yield of 4.5 percent. Lucky you. Pat yourself on the back.

P/E

REMEMBER

The *price-to-earnings ratio* (P/E ratio, for short) is the relationship between the price of a stock and the company's earnings. P/E ratios are widely followed and are important barometers of value in the world of stock investing. The P/E ratio (also called the *earnings multiple* or just *multiple*) is frequently used to determine whether a stock is expensive (a good value). Value investors (such as yours truly) find P/E ratios to be essential to analyzing a stock as a potential investment. As a general rule, the P/E should be 10 to 20 for large-cap or income stocks. For growth stocks, a P/E no greater than 30 to 40 is preferable. (See Chapter 6 for full details on P/E ratios.)

In the P/E ratios reported in stock tables, *price* refers to the cost of a single share of stock. *Earnings* refers to the company's reported earnings per share as of the most recent four quarters. The P/E ratio is the price divided by the earnings. In Table 6-1, VNI has a reported P/E of 12, which is considered a low P/E. Notice how SHC has a relatively high P/E (76). This stock is considered too pricey because you're paying a price equivalent to 76 times earnings.

Also notice that DBC has no available P/E ratio. Usually, this lack of a P/E ratio indicates that the company reported a loss in the most recent four quarters.

Day last

The "Day Last" column tells you how trading ended for a particular stock on the day represented by the table. In Table 6-1, LDI ended the most recent day of trading at $41. Some newspapers report the high and low for that day in addition to the stock's ending price for the day.

Net change

The information in the "Net Chg" column answers the question, "How did the stock price end today compared with its price at the end of the prior trading day?" Table 6-1 shows that SHC stock ended the trading day up 25 cents (at $21.25). This column tells you that SHC ended the prior day at $21. VNI ended the day at $22 (up 10 cents), so you can tell that the prior trading day it ended at $21.90.

Using News about Dividends

Reading and understanding the news about dividends is essential if you're an income investor. The following sections explain some basics you should know about dividends.

TIP

You can find news and information on dividends in websites for media such as *The Wall Street Journal* (www.wsj.com), *Investor's Business Daily* (www.investors.com), Nasdaq (www.nasdaq.com), MarketWatch (www.marketwatch.com), and *Barron's* (www.barrons.com).

Looking at important dates

REMEMBER

To understand how buying stocks that pay dividends can benefit you as an investor, you need to know how companies report and pay dividends. Some important dates in the life of a dividend are as follows:

>> **Date of declaration:** This is the date when a company reports a quarterly dividend and the subsequent payment

dates. On January 15, for example, a company may report that it "is pleased to announce a quarterly dividend of 50 cents per share to shareholders of record as of February 10." That was easy. The date of declaration is really just the announcement date. Whether you buy the stock before, on, or after the date of declaration doesn't matter in regard to receiving the stock's quarterly dividend. The date that matters is the date of record (see that bullet later in this list).

>> **Date of execution:** This is the day you actually initiate the stock transaction (buying or selling). If you call up a broker (or contact them online) today to buy (or sell) a particular stock, then today is the date of execution, or the date on which you execute the trade. You don't own the stock on the date of execution; it's just the day you put in the order. For an example, skip to the following section.

>> **Closing date (settlement date):** This is the date on which the trade is finalized, which usually happens one business day after the date of execution. The closing date for stock is similar in concept to a real estate closing. On the closing date, you're officially the proud new owner (or happy seller) of the stock.

>> **Ex-dividend date:** *Ex-dividend* means "without dividend." Because it takes one day to process a stock purchase before you become an official owner of the stock, you have to qualify (that is, you have to own or buy the stock) *before* the one-day period. That one-day period is referred to as the *ex-dividend period.* When you buy stock during this short time frame, you aren't on the books of record, because the closing (or settlement) date falls after the date of record. However, you will be able to buy the stock for a slighter lower price to offset the amount of the dividend. See the next section to see the effect that the ex-dividend date can have on an investor.

>> **Date of record:** This date is used to identify which stockholders qualify to receive the declared dividend. Because stock is bought and sold every day, how does the company know which investors to pay? The company establishes a cutoff date by declaring a date of record. All investors who are official stockholders as of the declared date of record receive the dividend on the payment date, even if they plan to sell the stock any time between the date of declaration and the date of record.

>> **Payment date:** The date on which a company issues and mails its dividend checks to shareholders. Finally!

For typical dividends, the events in Table 5-2 happen four times per year.

TABLE 5-2 **The Life of the Quarterly Dividend**

Event	Sample Date	Comments
Date of declaration	January 15	The date that the company declares the quarterly dividend
Ex-dividend date	February 9	Starts the one-day period during which, if you buy the stock, you don't qualify for the dividend
Date of record	February 10	The date by which you must be on the books of record to qualify for the dividend
Payment date	February 27	The date that payment is made (a dividend check is issued and mailed to stockholders who were on the books of record as of February 10)

Understanding why certain dates matter

REMEMBER

One business day passes between the date of execution and the closing date. One business day passes between the ex-dividend date and the date of record. This information is important to know if you want to qualify to receive an upcoming dividend. Timing is important, and if you understand these dates, you know when to purchase stock and whether you qualify for a dividend.

As an example, say that you want to buy ValueNowInc (VNI) in time to qualify for the quarterly dividend of 25 cents per share. Assume that the date of record (the date by which you have to be an official owner of the stock) is February 10. You have to execute the trade (buy the stock) no later than February 8 to be assured of the dividend. If you execute the trade right on February 9 (the ex-dividend date), you will not qualify for the dividend because settlement will occur after the date of record.

But what if you execute the trade on February 10, a day later? Well, the trade's closing date is February 11, which occurs *after* the date of record. Because you aren't on the books as an official stockholder on the date of record, you aren't getting that quarterly dividend. In this example, the February 9–10 period is called the *ex-dividend period*.

TIP

Fortunately, for those people who buy the stock during this brief ex-dividend period, the stock actually trades at a slightly lower price to reflect the amount of the dividend. If you can't get the dividend, you may as well save on the stock purchase. How's that for a silver lining?

Evaluating Investment Tips

Psst. Have I got a stock tip for you! Come closer. You know what it is? Research! What I'm trying to tell you is to never automatically invest just because you get a hot tip from someone. Good investment selection means looking at several sources before you decide on a stock. No shortcut exists. That said, getting opinions from others never hurts — just be sure to carefully analyze the information you get.

Here are some important points to bear in mind as you evaluate tips and advice from others:

>> **Consider the source.** Frequently, people buy stock based on the views of some market strategist or market analyst. People may see an analyst being interviewed on a TV financial show and take that person's opinions and advice as valid and good. The danger here is that the analyst may be biased because of some relationship that isn't disclosed on the show. Analysts are required to disclose conflicts of interest on business channels.

WARNING

It happens on TV all too often. The show's host interviews analyst U.R. Kiddingme from the investment firm Foollum & Sellum. The analyst says, "Implosion Corp. is a good buy with solid, long-term upside potential." You later find out that the analyst's employer gets investment banking fees from Implosion Corp. Do you really think that analyst would ever issue a negative report on a company that's helping to pay the bills? It's not likely.

>> **Get multiple views.** Don't base your investment decisions on just one source unless you have the best reasons in the

world for thinking that a particular, single source is outstanding and reliable. A better approach is to scour current issues of independent financial publications, such as *Barron's* or *Money* magazine, and other publications and websites.

» **Gather data from the SEC.** When you want to get more objective information about a company, why not take a look at the reports that firms must file with the SEC? These reports are the same reports that the pundits and financial reporters read. Arguably, the most valuable report you can look at is the 10-K. The 10-K is a report that all publicly traded companies must file with the SEC. It provides valuable information on the company's operations and financial data for the most recent year, and it's likely to be less biased than the information a company includes in other corporate reports, such as an annual report. The next most important document from the SEC is the 10-Q, which gives the investor similar detailed information but for a single quarter. (See Chapter 7 for more information about these documents.)

TIP

To access 10-K and 10-Q reports, go to the SEC's website (www.sec.gov). From there, you can find the SEC's extensive database of public filings called the Electronic Data Gathering, Analysis, and Retrieval system (EDGAR, for short). By searching EDGAR, you can find companies' balance sheets, income statements, and other related information so you can verify what others say and get a fuller picture of what a business is doing and what its financial condition is.

Chapter **6**

Choosing Winning Stocks with Basic Accounting

oo often, the only number investors look at when they look at a stock is the stock's price. Yet what determines the stock price is the company behind that single number. To make a truly good choice in the world of stocks, you have to consider the company's financial information. What does it take to see these important numbers?

This book, and a little work on your part, are all you need to succeed. This chapter takes the mystery out of the numbers behind the stock. The most tried-and-true method for picking a good stock starts with picking a good company. Picking a company means looking at its products, services, industry, and financial strength. Considering the problems that the market has witnessed in recent years — such as subprime debt problems and derivative meltdowns wreaking havoc on public companies and financial firms — this chapter is more important than ever. Understanding the basics behind the numbers can save your portfolio.

Recognizing Value When You See It

If you pick a stock based on the value of the underlying company that issues it, you're a *value investor* (an investor who looks at a company's value to judge whether you can purchase the stock at a good price). Companies have value the same way many things have value, such as eggs or elephant-foot umbrella stands. And there's a fair price to buy them at, too. Take eggs, for example. You can eat them and have a tasty treat while getting nutrition as well. But would you buy an egg for $1,000 (and no, you're not a starving millionaire on a desert island)? Of course not. But what if you could buy an egg for 5 cents? At that point, it has value *and* a good price. This kind of deal is a value investor's dream.

Value investors analyze a company's *fundamentals* (sales, earnings, assets, net worth, and so on) to see whether the information justifies purchasing the stock. They see whether the stock price is low relative to these verifiable, quantifiable factors. Therefore, value investors use *fundamental analysis,* whereas other investors may use technical analysis. *Technical analysis* looks at stock charts and statistical data, such as trading volume and historical stock prices. Some investors use a combination of both strategies.

History has shown that the most successful long-term investors have typically been value investors using fundamental analysis as their primary investing approach. The most consistently successful long-term investors were — and are — predominantly value investors (yes, I count myself in this crowd as well).

In the following sections, I describe different kinds of value and explain how to spot a company's value in several places.

Understanding different types of value

Value may seem like a murky or subjective term, but it's the essence of good stock picking. You can measure value in different ways (as I explain in the following sections), so you need to know the differences and understand the impact that value has on your investment decisions.

Market value

When you hear someone quoting a stock at $47 per share, that price reflects the stock's market value. The total market valuation of a company's stock is also referred to as its *market cap* or *market capitalization*. How do you determine a company's market cap? With the following simple formula:

> Market capitalization = Share price × Number of shares outstanding

If Bolshevik Corp.'s stock is $35 per share, and it has 10 million shares outstanding (or the number of shares issued less Treasury shares), its market cap is $350 million. Granted, $350 million may sound like a lot of money, but Bolshevik Corp. is considered a small-cap stock (see Chapter 1).

Who sets the market value of stock? The market, of course! Millions of investors buying and selling directly and through intermediaries such as mutual funds determine the market value of any particular stock. If the market perceives that the company is desirable, investor demand for the company's stock pushes up the share price.

The problem with market valuation is that it's not always a good indicator of a good investment. In recent years, plenty of companies have had astronomical market values, yet they've proven to be very risky investments. For example, think about a company that was set to go public (in an initial public offering [IPO]) in 2019. WeWork was expected to have a market value (before going public) as high as $47 billion. Investors such as you and I couldn't obtain complete financial information on this highly anticipated company, but we assumed it was a big deal due to its multibillion-dollar market value and the involvement of notable financial institutions such as JPMorgan and SoftBank. Hey, what could go wrong? After the discovery of financial difficulties and large losses, WeWork's IPO was canceled, and the market value totally evaporated and hit zero. Yikes! Because market value is a direct result of buying and selling by stock investors, it can be a fleeting thing. This precariousness is why investors must understand the company behind the stock price and its market valuation.

Book value and intrinsic value

Book value (also referred to as *accounting value*) looks at a company from a balance-sheet perspective (assets minus liabilities equals net worth, or *stockholders' equity*). It's a way of judging a firm by its net worth to see whether the stock's market value is reasonable compared to the company's intrinsic value. *Intrinsic value* is tied to what the market price of a company's assets — both *tangible* (such as equipment) and *intangible* (such as patents) — would be if they were sold.

REMEMBER

Generally, market value tends to be higher than book value. If market value is substantially higher than book value, the value investor becomes more reluctant to buy that particular stock because it's overvalued. The closer the stock's market capitalization is to the book value, the safer the investment.

WARNING

I like to be cautious with a stock whose market value is more than five times its book value. If, for example, the market value is north of $2 billion and the book value is less than $500 million, that's a good indicator that the business may be *overvalued* (valued at a higher price than its book value and ability to generate a profit). Just understand that the farther the market value is from the company's book value, the more you'll pay for the company's real potential value. And the more you pay for the company's real value, the greater the risk that the company's market value (the stock price, that is) can decrease.

Sales value and earnings value

A company's intrinsic value is directly tied to its ability to make money. For this reason, many analysts like to value stocks from the perspective of the company's income statement. Two common barometers of value are expressed in ratios: the price-to-sales ratio (PSR) and the price-to-earnings (P/E) ratio. In both instances, the price is a reference to the company's market value (as reflected in its share price). Sales and earnings are references to the firm's ability to make money. I cover these two ratios more fully in the later section "Tooling around with ratios."

REMEMBER

For investors, the general approach is clear. The closer the market value is to the company's intrinsic value, the better. And, of course, if the market value is lower than the company's intrinsic value, you have a potential bargain worthy of a closer look. Part of looking closer means examining the company's income statement (which I discuss later in this chapter), also called the *profit-and-loss statement*, or simply the *P&L*. A low PSR is 1, a medium PSR is between 1 and 2, and a high PSR is 3 or higher.

Putting the pieces together

When you look at a company from a value-oriented perspective, here are some of the most important items to consider (see the later section "Accounting for Value" for more information):

>> **The balance sheet, to figure out the company's net worth:** A value investor doesn't buy a company's stock because it's cheap; they buy it because it's *undervalued* (the company is worth more than the price its stock reflects — its market value is as close as possible to its book value).

>> **The income statement, to figure out the company's profitability:** A company may be undervalued from a simple comparison of the book value and the market value, but that doesn't mean it's a screaming buy. For example, what if you find out that a company is in trouble and losing money this year? Do you buy its stock then? No, you don't. Why invest in the stock of a losing company? (If you do, you aren't investing — you're gambling or speculating.) The heart of a firm's value, besides its net worth, is its ability to generate profit.

>> **Ratios that let you analyze just how well (or not so well) the company is doing:** Value investors basically look for a bargain. That being the case, they generally don't look at companies that everyone is talking about, because by that point, the stock of those companies ceases to be a bargain. The value investor searches for a stock that will eventually be discovered by the market and then watches as the stock price goes up. But before you bother digging into the fundamentals to find that bargain stock, first make sure that the company is making money.

The more ways that you can look at a company and see value, the better:

>> **Examine the P/E ratio.** The first thing I look at is the P/E ratio. Does the company have one? (This question may sound dumb, but if the company is losing money, it may not have one.) Does the P/E ratio look reasonable or is it in triple-digit, nosebleed territory?

>> **Check out the debt load.** Next, look at the company's *debt load* (the total amount of liabilities). Is it less than the company's equity? Are sales healthy and increasing from the prior year? Does the firm compare favorably in these categories versus other companies in the same industry?

TIP

>> **Think in terms of tens.** Simplicity to me is best. You'll notice that the number 10 comes up frequently as I measure a company's performance, juxtaposing all the numbers that you need to be aware of. If net income is rising by 10 percent or more, that's fine. If the company is in the top 10 percent of its industry, that's great. If the industry is growing by 10 percent or better (sales and so on), that's terrific. If sales are up 10 percent or more from the prior year, that's wonderful. A great company doesn't have to have all these things going for it, but it should have as many of these things happening as possible to ensure greater potential success.

Does every company/industry have to neatly fit these criteria? No, of course not. But it doesn't hurt you to be as picky as possible. You need to find only a handful of stocks from thousands of choices. (Hey, this approach has worked for me, my clients, and my students for more than three decades — 'nuff said.)

TIP

Value investors can find thousands of companies that have value, but they can probably buy only a handful at a truly good price. The number of stocks that can be bought at a good price is relative to the market. In mature *bull markets* (markets in a prolonged period of rising prices), a good price is hard to find because most stocks have probably seen significant price increases, but in *bear markets* (markets in a prolonged period of falling prices), good companies at bargain prices are easier to come by.

Accounting for Value

Profit is to a company what oxygen is to you and me. Without profit, a company can't survive, much less thrive. Without profit, it can't provide jobs, pay taxes, and invest in new products, equipment, or innovation. Without profit, the company eventually goes bankrupt, and the price of its stock plummets toward zero.

In the heady days leading up to the bear market of 2008–2009, many investors lost a lot of money simply because they invested in stocks of companies that weren't making a profit. Lots of public companies ended up like bugs that just didn't see the windshield coming their way. Companies such as Bear Stearns entered the graveyard of rather-be-forgotten stocks. Stock investors as a group lost trillions of dollars investing in glitzy companies that sounded good but weren't making money. When their brokers were saying, "Buy, buy, buy," their hard-earned money was saying, "Bye, bye, bye!" What were they thinking?

Stock investors need to pick up some rudimentary knowledge of accounting to round out their stock-picking prowess and to be sure that they're getting a good value for their investment dollars. Accounting is the language of business. If you don't understand basic accounting, you'll have difficulty being a successful investor. Investing without accounting knowledge is like traveling without a map. However, if you can run a household budget, using accounting analysis to evaluate stocks is easier than you think, as you find out in the following sections.

TIP

Finding the relevant financial data on a company isn't difficult in the age of information and 24-hour internet access. Websites such as www.nasdaq.com can give you the most recent balance sheets and income statements of most public companies. You can find out more about public information and company research in Chapter 5.

Breaking down the balance sheet

REMEMBER

A company's balance sheet gives you a financial snapshot of what the company looks like in terms of the following equation:

Assets – Liabilities = Net worth (or net equity)

In the following sections, I list the questions that a balance sheet can answer and explain how to judge a company's strength over time from a balance sheet.

Answering a few balance sheet questions

Analyze the following items that you find on the balance sheet:

>> **Total assets:** Have they increased from the prior year? If not, was it because of the sale of an asset or a write-off (uncollectable accounts receivable, for example)?

» **Financial assets:** In recent years, many companies (especially banks and brokerage firms) had questionable financial assets (such as subprime mortgages and specialized bonds) that went bad, and they had to write them off as unrecoverable losses. Does the company you're analyzing have a large exposure to financial assets that are low-quality (and, hence, risky) debt?

» **Inventory:** Is inventory higher or lower than last year? If sales are flat but inventory is growing, that may be a problem.

» **Debt:** Debt is the biggest weakness on the corporate balance sheet. Make sure that debt isn't a growing item and that it's under control. In recent years, debt has become a huge problem.

» **Derivatives:** A *derivative* is a speculative and complex financial instrument that doesn't constitute ownership of an asset (such as a stock, bond, or commodity) but is a promise to convey ownership. Some derivatives are quite acceptable because they're used as protective or hedging vehicles (this use isn't my primary concern). However, they're frequently used to generate income and can then carry risks that can increase liabilities. Standard options and futures are examples of derivatives on a regulated exchange, but the derivatives I'm talking about here are a different animal and in an unregulated part of the financial world. They have a book value exceeding $600 trillion and can easily devastate a company, sector, or market (as the credit crisis of 2008 showed).

WARNING

Find out whether the company dabbles in these complicated, dicey, leveraged financial instruments. Find out from the company's 10-K report (see Chapter 7) whether it has derivatives and, if so, the total amount. Having derivatives that are valued higher than the company's net equity may cause tremendous problems. Derivatives problems sank many organizations ranging from stodgy banks (Barings Bank of England) to affluent counties (Orange County, California) to once-respected hedge funds (LTCM) to infamous corporations (Enron in 2001 and Glencore in 2015).

» **Equity:** *Equity* is the company's net worth (what's left in the event that all the assets are used to pay off all the company debts). The stockholders' equity should be increasing steadily by at least 10 percent per year. If not, find out why.

Table 6-1 shows you a brief example of a balance sheet.

TABLE 6-1 **XYZ Balance Sheet — December 31, 2022**

Assets (What the Company Owns)	Amount
1. Cash and inventory	$5,000
2. Equipment and other assets	$7,000
3. TOTAL ASSETS (Item 1 plus Item 2)	$12,000
Liabilities (What the Company Owes)	Amount
4. Short-term debt	$1,500
5. Other debt	$2,500
6. TOTAL LIABILITIES (Item 4 plus Item 5)	$4,000
7. NET EQUITY (Item 3 minus Item 6)	$8,000

By looking at a company's balance sheet, you can address the following questions:

>> **What does the company own (assets)?** The company can own assets, which can be financial, tangible, and/or intangible. An *asset* is anything that has value or that can be converted to or sold for cash. Financial assets can be cash, investments (such as stocks or bonds of other companies), or accounts receivable. Assets can be tangible items such as inventory, equipment, and/or buildings. They can also be intangible things such as licenses, trademarks, or copyrights.

>> **What does the company owe (liabilities)?** A *liability* is anything of value that the company must ultimately pay someone else for. Liabilities can be invoices (accounts payable) or short-term or long-term debt.

REMEMBER

>> **What is the company's net equity (net worth)?** After you subtract the liabilities from the assets, the remainder is called *net worth, net equity,* or *net stockholders' equity.* This number is critical when calculating a company's book value.

Assessing a company's financial strength over time

The logic behind the assets/liabilities relationship of a company is the same as that of your own household. When you look at a snapshot of your own finances (your personal balance sheet), how can you tell whether you're doing well? Odds are that you start by comparing some numbers. If your net worth is $5,000, you may say, "That's great!" But a more appropriate remark is something like, "That's great compared to, say, a year ago."

TIP

Compare a company's balance sheet at a recent point in time to a past time. You should do this comparative analysis with all the key items on the balance sheet, which I list in the preceding section, to see the company's progress (or lack thereof). Is it growing its assets and/or shrinking its debt? Most important, is the company's net worth growing? Has it grown by at least 10 percent since a year ago? All too often, investors stop doing their homework after they make an initial investment. You should continue to look at the firm's numbers regularly so that you can be ahead of the curve. If the business starts having problems, you can get out before the rest of the market starts getting out (which causes the stock price to fall).

To judge the financial strength of a company, ask yourself the following questions:

>> **Are the company's assets greater in value than they were three months ago, a year ago, or two years ago?** Compare current asset size to the most recent two years to make sure that the company is growing in size and financial strength.

>> **How do the individual items compare with prior periods?** Some particular assets that you want to take note of are cash, inventory, and accounts receivable.

>> **Are liabilities such as accounts payable and debt about the same, lower, or higher compared to prior periods? Are they growing at a similar, faster, or slower rate than the company's assets?** Debt that rises faster and higher than items on the other side of the balance sheet is a warning sign of pending financial problems.

>> **Is the company's net worth or equity greater than the preceding year? And is that year's equity greater than the year before?** In a healthy company, the net worth is constantly rising. As a general rule, in good economic times, net worth should be at least 10 percent higher than the preceding year. In tough economic times (such as a recession), 5 percent is acceptable. Seeing the net worth grow at a rate of 15 percent or higher is great.

Looking at the income statement

Where do you look if you want to find out what a company's profit is? Check out the firm's income statement. It reports, in detail, a simple accounting equation that you probably already know:

Sales – Expenses = Net profit (or net earnings, or net income)

Look at the following figures found on the income statement:

>> **Sales:** Are they increasing? If not, why not? By what percentage are sales increasing? Preferably, they should be 10 percent higher than the year before. Sales are, after all, where the money comes from to pay for all the company's activities (such as expenses) and create subsequent profits.

>> **Expenses:** Do you see any unusual items? Are total expenses reported higher than the prior year, and if so, by how much? If the total is significantly higher, why? A company with large, rising expenses will see profits suffer, which isn't good for the stock price.

>> **Research and development (R&D):** How much is the company spending on R&D? Companies that rely on new product development (such as pharmaceuticals or biotech firms) should spend at least as much as they did the year before (preferably more) because new products mean future earnings and growth.

>> **Earnings:** This figure reflects the bottom line. Are total earnings higher than the year before? How about earnings from operations (leaving out expenses such as taxes and interest)? The earnings section is the heart and soul of the income statement and of the company itself. Out of all the numbers in the financial statements, earnings have the greatest single impact on the company's stock price.

Table 6-2 shows you a brief example of an income statement.

Looking at the income statement, an investor can try to answer the following questions:

>> **What sales did the company make?** Businesses sell products and services that generate revenue (known as *sales* or *gross sales*). Sales also are referred to as the *top line*.

TABLE 6-2 XYZ Income Statement — December 31, 2022

Total Sales (Or Revenue)	Amount
1. Sales of products	$11,000
2. Sales of services	$3,000
3. TOTAL SALES (Item 1 plus Item 2)	$14,000
Expenses	**Amount**
4. Marketing and promotion	$2,000
5. Payroll costs	$9,000
6. Other costs	$1,500
7. TOTAL EXPENSES (Item 4 plus Item 5 plus Item 6)	$12,500
8. NET INCOME (Item 3 minus Item 7) (In this case, it's a net profit.)	$1,500

>> **What expenses did the company incur?** In generating sales, companies pay expenses such as payroll, utilities, advertising, administration, and so on.

>> **What is the net profit?** Also called *net earnings* or *net income*, net profit is the *bottom line*. After paying for all expenses, what profit did the company make?

The information you glean should give you a strong idea about a firm's current financial strength and whether it's successfully increasing sales, holding down expenses, and ultimately maintaining profitability. You can find out more about sales, expenses, and profits in the following sections.

Sales

Sales refers to the money that a company receives as customers buy its goods and/or services. It's a simple item on the income statement and a useful number to look at. Analyzing a business by looking at its sales is called *top-line analysis*.

As an investor, you should take into consideration the following points about sales:

>> **Sales should be increasing.** A healthy, growing company has growing sales. They should grow at least 10 percent

from the prior year, and you should look at the most recent three years.

>> **Core sales (sales of those products or services that the company specializes in) should be increasing.** Frequently, the sales figure has a lot of stuff lumped into it. Maybe the company sells widgets (what the heck is a widget, anyway?), but the core sales shouldn't include other things, such as the sale of a building or other unusual items. Take a close look. Isolate the firm's primary offerings and ask whether these sales are growing at a reasonable rate (such as 10 percent).

>> **Does the company have odd items or odd ways of calculating sales?** In the late 1990s, many companies boosted their sales by aggressively offering affordable financing with easy repayment terms. Say you find out that Suspicious Sales, Inc., had annual sales of $50 million, reflecting a 25 percent increase from the year before. Looks great! But what if you find out that $20 million of that sales number comes from sales made on credit that the company extended to buyers? Some companies that use this approach later have to write off losses as uncollectable debt because the customers ultimately can't pay for the goods.

TIP

If you want to get a good clue as to whether a company is artificially boosting sales, check its accounts receivable (listed in the asset section of its balance sheet). *Accounts receivable* refers to money that is owed to the company for goods that customers have purchased on credit. If you find out that sales went up by $10 million (great!) but accounts receivable went up by $20 million (uh-oh), something just isn't right. That may be a sign that the financing terms were too easy, and the company may have a problem collecting payment (especially in a recession).

Expenses

How much a company spends has a direct relationship to its profitability. If spending isn't controlled or held at a sustainable level, it may spell trouble for the business.

When you look at a company's expense items, consider the following:

>> **Compare expense items to the prior period.** Are expenses higher than, lower than, or about the same as those from

the prior period? If the difference is significant, you should see commensurate benefits elsewhere. In other words, if overall expenses are 10 percent higher compared to the prior period, are sales at least 10 percent more during the same period?

>> **Are some expenses too high?** Look at the individual expense items. Are they significantly higher than the year before? If so, why?

>> **Have any unusual items been expensed?** An unusual expense isn't necessarily a negative. Expenses may be higher than usual if a company writes off uncollectable accounts receivable as a bad debt expense. Doing so inflates the total expenses and subsequently results in lower earnings. Pay attention to nonrecurring charges that show up on the income statement and determine whether they make sense.

Profit

Earnings or profit is the single most important item on the income statement. It's also the one that receives the most attention in the financial media. When a company makes a profit, it's usually reported in both absolute dollars and as earnings per share (EPS). So, if you hear that XYZ Corporation (yes, the infamous XYZ Corp.!) beat last quarter's earnings by a penny, here's how to translate that news. Suppose that the company made $1 per share this quarter and 99 cents per share last quarter. If that company had 100 million shares of stock outstanding, its profit this quarter is $100 million (the EPS × the number of shares outstanding), which is $1 million more than it made in the prior quarter ($1 million is 1 cent per share × 100 million shares).

TIP

Don't simply look at current earnings as an isolated figure. Always compare current earnings to earnings in past periods (usually a year). For example, if you're looking at a retailer's fourth-quarter results, don't compare them with the retailer's third-quarter outcome. Doing so is like comparing apples to oranges. What if the company usually does well during the December holidays but poorly in the fall? In that case, you don't get a fair comparison.

A strong company should show consistent earnings growth from the period before (such as the prior year or the same quarter from the prior year), and you should check the period before that, too, so you can determine whether earnings are consistently rising over time. Earnings growth is an important barometer of the company's potential growth and bodes well for the stock price.

When you look at earnings, here are some things to consider:

>> **Total earnings:** This item is the most watched. Total earnings should grow year to year by at least 10 percent.

>> **Operational earnings:** Break down the total earnings, and look at a key subset — that portion of earnings derived from the company's core activity. Is the company continuing to make money from its primary goods and services?

>> **Nonrecurring items:** Are earnings higher (or lower) than usual or than expected, and if so, why? Frequently, the difference results from items such as the sale of an asset or a large depreciation write-off.

TIP

I like to keep percentages as simple as possible. Ten percent is a good number because it's easy to calculate, and it's a good benchmark. However, 5 percent isn't unacceptable if you're talking about tough times, such as a recession. Obviously, if sales, earnings, and/or net worth are hitting or surpassing 15 percent, that's great.

Tooling around with ratios

A *ratio* is a helpful numerical tool that you can use to find out the relationship between two or more figures found in a company's financial data. A ratio can add meaning to a number or put it in perspective. Ratios sound complicated, but they're easier to understand than you may think.

Say that you're considering a stock investment and the company you're looking at has earnings of $1 million this year. You may think that's a nice profit, but in order for this amount to be meaningful, you have to compare it to something. What if you find out that the other companies in the industry (of similar size and scope) had earnings of $500 million? Does that change your thinking? Or what if the same company had earnings of $75 million in the prior period? Does that change your mind?

Two key ratios to be aware of are

>> Price-to-earnings (P/E) ratio
>> Price to sales ratio (PSR)

Every investor wants to find stocks that have a 20 percent average growth rate over the past five years and have a low P/E ratio (sounds like a dream). Use stock-screening tools available for free on the internet to do your research. A *stock-screening tool* lets you plug in numbers (such as sales or earnings) and ratios (such as the P/E ratio or the debt-to-equity ratio) and then — click! — up come stocks that fit your criteria. These tools are a good starting point for serious investors. Many brokers have them on their websites (such as Charles Schwab at www.schwab.com and E*TRADE at www.etrade.com). You can also find some excellent stock screening tools at Yahoo! Finance (https://finance.yahoo.com), Bloomberg (www.bloomberg.com), Nasdaq (www.nasdaq.com), and MarketWatch (www.marketwatch.com).

The P/E ratio

The *price-to-earnings ratio* is very important in analyzing a potential stock investment because it's one of the most widely regarded barometers of a company's value, and it's usually reported along with the company's stock price in the financial page listing. The major significance of the P/E ratio is that it establishes a direct relationship between the bottom line of a company's operations — the earnings (or net profit) — and the stock price.

The *P* in P/E stands for the stock's current price, and the *E* is for earnings per share (typically, the most recent 12 months of earnings). The P/E ratio is also referred to as the *earnings multiple* or just *multiple*.

You calculate the P/E ratio by dividing the price of the stock by the earnings per share. If the price of a single share of stock is $10 and the earnings (on a per-share basis) are $1, then the P/E is 10. If the stock price goes to $35 per share and the earnings are unchanged, then the P/E is 35. Basically, the higher the P/E, the more you pay for the company's earnings.

Why would you buy stock in one company with a relatively high P/E ratio instead of investing in another company with a lower P/E ratio? Keep in mind that investors buy stocks based on expectations. They may bid up the price of the stock (subsequently raising the stock's P/E ratio) because they feel that the company will have increased earnings in the near future. Perhaps they feel that the company has great potential (a pending new invention or lucrative business deal) that will eventually make it more profitable.

More profitability, in turn, has a beneficial impact on the firm's stock price. The danger with a high P/E is that if the company doesn't achieve the hoped-for results, the stock price can fall.

TIP

You should look at two types of P/E ratios to get a balanced picture of the company's value:

>> **Trailing P/E:** This P/E is the most frequently quoted because it deals with existing data. The trailing P/E uses the most recent 12 months of earnings in its calculation.

>> **Forward P/E:** This P/E is based on projections or expectations of earnings in the coming 12-month period. Although this P/E may seem preferable because it looks into the near future, it's still considered an estimate that may or may not prove to be accurate.

The following example illustrates the importance of the P/E ratio. Say you want to buy a business, and I'm selling a business. You come to me and say, "What do you have to offer?" I say, "Have I got a deal for you! I operate a retail business downtown that sells spatulas. The business nets a cool $2,000 profit per year." You reluctantly say, "Uh, okay, what's the asking price for the business?" I reply, "You can have it for only $1 million! What do you say?"

If you're sane, odds are that you politely turn down that offer. Even though the business is profitable (a cool $2,000 a year), you'd be crazy to pay a million bucks for it. In other words, the business is way overvalued (too expensive for what you're getting in return for your investment dollars). The million dollars would generate a better rate of return elsewhere and probably with less risk. As for the business, the P/E ratio of 500 ($1 million ÷ $2,000) is outrageous. This is definitely a case of an overvalued company — and a lousy investment.

What if I offered the business for $12,000? Does that price make more sense? Yes. The P/E ratio is a more reasonable 6 ($12,000 ÷ $2,000). In other words, the business pays for itself in about 6 years (versus 500 years in the prior example).

REMEMBER

Looking at the P/E ratio offers a shortcut for investors asking the question, "Is this stock overvalued?" As a general rule, the lower the P/E, the safer (or more conservative) the stock is. The reverse is more noteworthy: The higher the P/E, the greater the risk.

When someone refers to a P/E as high or low, you have to ask the question, "Compared to what?" A P/E of 30 is considered very high for a large-cap electric utility but quite reasonable for a small-cap, high-tech firm. Keep in mind that phrases such as *large cap* and *small cap* are just a reference to the company's market value or size (see Chapter 1 for details). *Cap* is short for *capitalization* (the total number of shares of stock outstanding × the share price).

The following basic points can help you evaluate P/E ratios:

>> **Compare a company's P/E ratio with its industry.** Electric utility industry stocks, for example, generally have a P/E that hovers in the 9–14 range. Therefore, an electric utility with a P/E of 45 indicates that something is wrong with that utility. (I touch on sectors and industries in Chapter 12.)

>> **Compare a company's P/E with the general market.** If you're looking at a small-cap stock on the Nasdaq that has a P/E of 100, and if the average P/E for established companies on the Nasdaq is 40, find out why. You should also compare the stock's P/E ratio with the P/E ratio for major indexes such as the Dow Jones Industrial Average (DJIA), the Standard & Poor's 500 (S&P 500), and the Nasdaq Composite. Stock indexes are useful for getting the big picture, and I include them in Chapter 11.

>> **Compare a company's current P/E with recent periods (such as this year versus last year).** If it currently has a P/E ratio of 20 and it previously had a P/E ratio of 30, you know that either the stock price has declined or earnings have risen. In this case, the stock is less likely to fall. That bodes well for the stock.

>> **Low P/E ratios aren't necessarily a sign of a bargain.** But if you're looking at a stock for many other reasons that seem positive (solid sales, strong industry, and so on) and it also has a low P/E, that's a good sign.

>> **High P/E ratios aren't necessarily bad.** But they do mean that you should investigate further. If a company is weak and the industry is shaky, heed the high P/E as a warning sign. Frequently, a high P/E ratio means that investors have bid up a stock price, anticipating future income. The problem is that if the anticipated income doesn't materialize, the stock price can fall.

>> **Watch out for a stock that doesn't have a P/E ratio.** In other words, it may have a price (the *P*), but it doesn't have earnings (the *E*). No earnings means no P/E, meaning that you're better off avoiding the stock. Can you still make money buying a stock with no earnings? Yes, but in that case you aren't investing; you're speculating.

The PSR

The *price-to-sales ratio* is a company's stock price divided by its sales. Because the sales number is rarely expressed as a per-share figure, it's easier to divide a company's total market value (see the "Market value" section, earlier in this chapter) by its total sales for the last 12 months.

As a general rule, stock trading at a PSR of 1 or less is a reasonably priced stock worthy of your attention. For example, say that a company has sales of $1 billion, and the stock has a total market value of $950 million. In that case, the PSR is 0.95. In other words, you can buy $1 of the company's sales for only 95 cents. All things being equal, that stock may be a bargain.

Analysts frequently use the PSR as an evaluation tool in the following circumstances:

>> In tandem with other ratios to get a more well-rounded picture of the company and the stock.

>> When they want an alternative way to value a business that doesn't have earnings.

>> When they want a true picture of the company's financial health, because sales are tougher for companies to manipulate than earnings.

>> When they're considering a company offering products (versus services). PSR is more suitable for companies that sell items that are easily counted (such as products). Firms that make their money through loans, such as banks, aren't usually valued with a PSR because deriving a usable PSR for them is more difficult.

Compare the company's PSR with other companies in the same industry, along with the industry average, so you get a better idea of the company's relative value.

IN THIS CHAPTER

» Paging through an annual report

» Reviewing other information sources for a second opinion

» Organizing your own research library

Chapter **7**

Deciphering Company Documents to Pick Stocks

inancial documents — good grief! Some people would rather suck a hospital mop than read some dry corporate or government report. Yet if you're serious about choosing stocks, you should be serious about your research. Fortunately, it's not as bad as you think (put away that disgusting mop). When you see that some basic research helps you build wealth, it gets easier.

In this chapter, I discuss the basic documents that you come across (or should come across) most often in your investing life. These documents include essential information that all investors need to know, not only at the time of the initial investment decision, but also for as long as that stock remains in their portfolio.

REMEMBER

If you plan to hold a stock for the long haul, reading the annual report and other reports covered in this chapter will be very helpful. If you intend to get rid of the stock soon or plan to hold it only for the short term, reading these reports diligently isn't that important.

A Message from the Bigwigs: Reading the Annual Report

When you're a regular stockholder, the company sends you its annual report. If you're not already a stockholder, contact the company's shareholder services (or investor relations) department for a hard copy or to get a copy emailed to you. Virtually all the websites for public companies have publicly filed documents or links to where they can be found at the Securities and Exchange Commission (SEC).

You can also often view a company's annual report at its website. Any major search engine can help you find it. Downloading or printing the annual report is easy.

TIP

The following resources also provide access to annual reports:

>> **Check out The Public Register's Annual Report Service.** Go to http://prars.com to order a hard copy or to www.annualreportservice.com to view reports online. This organization maintains an extensive collection of annual reports.

>> **Use the free annual report service of *The Wall Street Journal.*** If you read the newspaper's financial pages and see a company with the club symbol (like the one you see on a playing card), then you can order that company's annual report by visiting the website (www.wsj.com).

You need to carefully analyze an annual report to find out the following:

>> **How well the company is doing:** Are earnings higher, lower, or the same as the year before? How are sales doing? You can find these numbers clearly presented in the annual report's financial section.

>> **Whether the company is making more money than it's spending:** How does the balance sheet look? Are assets higher or lower than the year before? Is debt growing, shrinking, or about the same as the year before? For more details on balance sheets, see Chapter 6.

>> **What management's strategic plan is for the coming year:** How will management build on the company's success? This plan is usually covered in the beginning of the annual report — frequently in the letter from the chairman of the board.

Your task boils down to figuring out where the company has been, where it is now, and where it's going. As an investor, you don't need to read the annual report like a novel — from cover to cover. Instead, approach it like a newspaper and jump around to the relevant sections to get the answers you need to decide whether you should buy or hold onto the stock. I describe the makeup of the annual report and proxy materials in the following sections.

Analyzing the annual report's anatomy

Not every company puts its annual report together in exactly the same way — the style of presentation varies. Some annual reports have gorgeous graphics or coupons for the company's products, whereas others are in a standard black-and-white typeface with no cosmetic frills at all. But every annual report does include common basic content, such as the income statement and the balance sheet. The following sections present typical components of an average annual report. (Keep in mind that not every annual report presents the sections in the same order.)

The letter from the chairman of the board

The first thing you see is usually the letter from the chairman of the board. It's the "Dear Stockholder" letter that communicates views from the head muckety-muck. The chairman's letter is designed to put the best possible perspective on the company's operations during the past year. Be aware of this bias; no one in upper management wants to panic stockholders. If the company is doing well, the letter will certainly point it out. If the company is having hard times, the letter will probably put a positive spin on the company's difficulties. If the *Titanic* had had an annual report, odds are, the last letter would have reported, "Great news! A record number of our customers participated in our spontaneous moonlight swimming program. In addition, we confidently project no operating expenses whatsoever for the subsequent fiscal quarter." You get the point.

To get a good idea of what issues the company's management team feels are important and what goals it wants to accomplish, keep the following questions in mind:

>> What does the letter say about changing conditions in the company's business? How about in the industry?

>> If any difficulties exist, does the letter communicate a clear and logical action plan (cutting costs, closing money-losing plants, and so on) to get the company back on a positive track?

>> What's being highlighted and why? For example, is the firm focusing on research and development for new products or on a new deal with China?

>> Does the letter offer apologies for anything the company did? If, for example, it fell short of sales expectations, does the letter offer a reason for the shortcoming?

>> Did the company make (or will it make) new acquisitions or major developments (say, selling products to China or a new marketing agreement with a Fortune 500 company)?

TIP

Read an annual report (or any messages from upper management) in the same way you read or hear anything from a politician — be more concerned with means than ends. In other words, don't tell me what the goal is (greater profitability or peace on earth); tell me how you're going to get there. Executives may say, "We will increase sales and profits," but saying "We will increase sales and profits by doing X, Y, and Z" is a better message because you can then decide for yourself whether the road map makes sense.

The company's offerings

This section of an annual report can have various titles (such as "Sales and Marketing"), but it generally covers what the company sells. You should understand the products or services (or both) that the business sells and why customers purchase them. If you don't understand what the company offers, then understanding how it earns money, which is the driving force behind its stock, is more difficult.

Are the company's core or primary offerings selling well? If, for example, the earnings of McDonald's are holding steady but earnings strictly from burgers and fries are fizzling, that's a cause for concern. If a business ceases making money from its specialty, you should be cautious. Here are some other questions to ask:

» How does the company distribute its offerings? Through a website, malls, representatives, or some other means? Does it sell only to the U.S. market, or is its distribution international? Generally, the greater the distribution, the greater the potential sales and, ultimately, the higher the stock price.

» Are most of the company's sales to a definable marketplace? For example, if most of the sales are to a war-torn or politically unstable country, you should worry. If the company's customers aren't doing well, that has a direct impact on the company and, eventually, its stock.

» How are sales doing versus market standards? In other words, is the company doing better than the industry average? Is it a market leader in what it offers? The firm should be doing better than (or as well as) its peers in the industry. If the company is falling behind its competitors, that doesn't bode well for the stock in the long run.

» Does the report include information on the company's competitors and related matters? You should know who the company's competitors are because they have a direct effect on the company's success. If customers are choosing the competitor over your firm, the slumping sales and earnings will ultimately hurt the stock's price.

Financial statements

Look over the various financial statements and find the relevant numbers. Every annual report should have (at the very least) a balance sheet (for the beginning of the year and the end of year), three years (typically) of income statements, and cash flow statements for the years in question. Catching the important numbers on a financial statement isn't that difficult to do. However, it certainly helps when you pick up some basic accounting knowledge. Chapter 6 can give you more details on evaluating financial statements.

First, review the *income statement* (also known as the *profit-and-loss statement*, or simply *P&L*). It gives you the company's sales, expenses, and results (net income or net loss).

Next, look at the *balance sheet*. It provides a snapshot of a point in time (annual reports are required to provide two years of year-end balance sheets) that tells you what the company owns (its *assets*), what it owes (its *liabilities*), and the end result (its *net worth*). For a healthy company, assets should always be greater than liabilities.

Carefully read the footnotes to the financial statements. Sometimes big changes are communicated in small print. In current times, especially be wary of small print pointing out other debt or derivatives. *Derivatives* are complicated and (lately) very risky vehicles. Problems with derivatives were one of the major causes of the market turmoil that destroyed financial firms on Wall Street during late 2008. AIG, for example, is a major insurer that had to be bailed out by the Federal Reserve before it went bankrupt (shareholders suffered huge losses).

Derivatives are a huge land mine, and large money center banks still carry them. According to the Bank for International Settlements (www.bis.org), major money center banks are carrying more than 1 quadrillion dollars' worth of derivatives. (Whew! Now I see why they give away so many toasters.) Derivatives are especially worth being aware of if you're considering bank or other financial stocks for your portfolio.

Summary of past financial figures

The summary of past financial figures gives you a snapshot of the company's overall long-term progress. How many years does the annual report summarize? Some reports summarize three years, but most go back two years.

Management issues

The annual report's management issues section includes a reporting of current trends and issues, such as new developments happening in the industry that affect the company. See whether you agree with management's assessment of economic and market conditions that affect the firm's prospects. What significant developments in society does management perceive as affecting the company's operations? Does the report include information on current or pending lawsuits?

CPA opinion letter

Annual reports typically include comments from the company's independent accounting firm. It may be an opinion letter or a simple paragraph with the accounting firm's views regarding the financial statements.

The CPA opinion letter offers an opinion about the accuracy of the financial data presented and information on how the statements were prepared. Check to see whether the letter includes any footnotes regarding changes in certain numbers or how they were reported. For example, a company that wants to report higher earnings may use a conservative method of measuring depreciation rather than a more aggressive approach. In any case, you should verify the numbers by looking at the company's 10-K document filed with the SEC (I describe this document in more detail later in this chapter).

Company identity data

The company identity data section informs you about the company's subsidiaries (or lesser businesses that it owns), brands, and addresses. It also contains standard data such as the headquarters' location and names of directors and officers. Many reports also include data on the directors' and officers' positions in stock ownership at year's end.

Stock data

The stock data section may include a history of the stock price, along with information such as what exchange the stock is listed on, the stock symbol, the company's dividend reinvestment plan (if any), and so on. It also includes information on stockholder services and who to contact for more information.

Going through the proxy materials

As a shareholder (or stockholder — same thing), you're entitled to vote at the annual shareholders meeting. If you ever get the opportunity to attend one, do so. You get to meet other shareholders and ask questions of management and other company representatives. Usually, the shareholder services department (or investor relations department) provides you with complete details. At the meetings, shareholders vote on company matters, such as approving a new accounting firm or deciding whether a proposed merger with another company will go forward.

If you can't attend (which is usually true for the majority of shareholders), you can vote by proxy. *Voting by proxy* essentially means that you vote by mail or electronically. You indicate your votes on the proxy statement (or card) and authorize a representative to vote at the meeting on your behalf. The proxy statement is usually sent to all shareholders, along with the annual report, just before the meeting.

Dig Deeper: Getting a Second Opinion

A wealth of valuable information is available for your investing pursuits. The resources in this section are just a representative few — a good representation, though. To get a more balanced view of the company and its prospects (instead of relying only on the annual report that I describe in the preceding section), take a look at several different sources of information for the stocks you're researching.

TIP

The information and research they provide can be expensive if you buy or subscribe on your own, but fortunately, most of the resources mentioned are usually available in the business reference section of a well-stocked public library.

Company documents filed with the SEC

Serious investors don't overlook the wealth of information that they can cull from documents filed with the SEC. Take the time and effort to review the documents in the following sections because they offer great insight regarding a company's activities.

Here's how to obtain the main documents that investors should be aware of:

>> **Drop by the company itself.** Stockholder services departments keep these publicly available documents on hand and usually give them out at no cost to interested parties.

>> **Visit the SEC, either in person or online.** These documents are available for public viewing at the SEC offices. You can find out more by contacting the Securities and Exchange Commission, Publications Unit, 450 Fifth St. NW, Washington, DC 20549.

TIP

At the SEC's website (www.sec.gov), you can check out the Electronic Data Gathering, Analysis, and Retrieval system (known as EDGAR) to search public documents filed. It's a tremendous source of documents that date back to 1994. You can search, print, or download documents very easily. Documents can be located either by document number or keyword search.

Form 10-K

Gee, how intimidating. Just the report name alone makes you scratch your head. To some people, 10-K refers to running a race of 10 kilometers. But if you're reading a 10-K, you may wish you were running one instead.

Form 10-K is a report that companies must file with the SEC annually. It works like the annual report that you get from the company, except that it provides more detailed financial information. It can be a little intimidating because the text can be dry and cumbersome. It's not exactly Shakespeare (although 10-K reports would've also driven Lady Macbeth insane); then again, the data isn't laden with as much spin as the annual report the company sends to shareholders. Without going crazy, go through each section of the 10-K. Take some extra time to scrutinize the section on financial data. Ask the same questions that you do when you're looking at the annual report.

TIP

The following websites can help you make sense of 10-K reports:

>> **Investopedia:** www.investopedia.com

>> **Investor.gov:** www.investor.gov

>> **Last10K.com:** https://last10k.com

>> **SEC Info:** www.secinfo.com

Form 10-Q

Form 10-Q is a quarterly report that gives you the same basic information as the 10-K, but it details only three months' worth of activity. Because a long time can pass between 10-Ks (after all, it is a year), don't wait 12 months to see how a company is progressing. Make a habit of seeing how the company is doing by comparing its recent 10-Q with one that covers the same quarter last year. Is the profit higher or lower? How about sales? Debt?

REMEMBER

Keep in mind that not every company has the same fiscal year. A company with a calendar year fiscal year (ending December 31), for example, files a 10-Q for each of the first three quarters and files a 10-K for the final quarter (the last three months of the year). The company reports its fourth-quarter data in the 10-K, along with the statistics for the full year.

Insider reports

Two types of insiders exist: those who work within a company and those outside the company who have a significant (5 percent or more) ownership of company stock. Tracking insider activity is very profitable for investors who want to follow in the footsteps of the people in the know.

REMEMBER

Every time an insider (such as the CEO or controller) buys or sells stock, the transaction has to be reported to the SEC. The insider actually reports the trade prior to transacting it. These reports are publicly available documents that allow you to see what the insiders are actually doing. Hearing what they say in public is one thing, but seeing what they're actually doing with their stock transactions is more important.

Value Line

The Value Line Investment Survey, one of many information products provided by Value Line Publishing, Inc., is considered a longtime favorite by many stock-investing professionals. You can look it over at any library that has a good business reference department. In the survey, Value Line covers the largest public companies and ranks them according to financial strength and several other key business factors. To get more information about Value Line, either head to the library or visit www.valueline.com.

Standard & Poor's

Another ubiquitous and venerable publisher is Standard & Poor's (S&P). Although it has a number of quality information products and services for both individual and institutional investors, the three you should take a look at are the following:

>> *S&P Stock Reports:* Available at many libraries, this guide comes out periodically and reports on stocks on the New York Stock Exchange (NYSE) and the largest firms listed on the Nasdaq. It gives a succinct, two-page summary of each stock, offering a snapshot of the company's current finances, along with a brief history and commentary on the company's activities. This guide also rates companies based on their financial strength.

>> **The S&P Industry Survey:** S&P gives detailed reports on the top industries, cramming a lot of information about a given industry in four to seven pages. This annual publication provides a nice summary of what's happened in each industry in the past 12 months, what the industry looks like today, and what the prospects are for the coming year. It also provides the important numbers (earnings, sales, and industry ranking) for the top 50 to 100 firms in each industry.

>> **S&P Bond Reports:** Yes, I know this book is about stocks. But a company's bond rating is invaluable for stock investors. S&P analyzes the strength of the bond issuer and ranks the bond for creditworthiness. If S&P gives a company a high rating, you have added assurance that the company is financially strong. You want the company to have a bond rating of AAA, AA, or A, because these ratings tell you that the company is "investment-grade."

Check out S&P's website at www.standardandpoors.com for more information about its publications.

Moody's Investment Service

Another stalwart publisher, Moody's offers vital research on stocks and bonds. *Moody's Handbook of Common Stocks* is usually available in the reference section of a well-stocked library. It offers stock and bond guides similar to S&P and also provides an independent bond-rating service. Check out www.moodys.com for more information.

TIP

A stock rated highly by both Moody's and S&P is a great choice for investors hunting for value investments.

Brokerage reports: The good, the bad, and the ugly

Clint Eastwood, where are you? Traditionally, brokerage reports have been a good source of information for investors seeking informed opinions about stocks. And they still are, but in recent years some brokers have been penalized for biased reports. Brokers should never be your sole source of information. (Otherwise, Clint may ask them whether they're feeling lucky, punks.) The following sections describe the good, the bad, and the ugly of brokerage reports.

The good

Research departments at brokerage firms provide stock reports and make them available for their clients and investment publications. The firms' analysts and market strategists generally prepare these reports. Good research is critical, and brokerage reports can be very valuable. What better source of guidance than full-time experts backed up by million-dollar research departments? Brokerage reports have some strong points:

>> The analysts are professionals who should understand the value of a company and its stock. They analyze and compare company data every day.

>> Analysts have at their disposal tremendous information and historical data that they can sift through to make informed decisions.

>> If you have an account with the firm, you can usually access the information at no cost.

The bad

WARNING

Well, brokerage reports may not be bad in every case, but at their worst, they're quite bad. Brokers make their money from commissions and investment banking fees (nothing bad here). However, they can find themselves in the awkward position of issuing brokerage reports on companies that are (or could be) customers of the brokerage firm that employs them (hmm — could be bad). Frequently, this relationship results in a brokerage report that paints an overly positive picture of a company that can be a bad investment (yup, that's bad). The bottom line is that you should always be wary of a conflict of interest when brokers are too pushy or optimistic about a particular security.

The ugly

During 1998–2000, an overwhelming number of brokerage reports issued glowing praise of companies that were either mediocre or dubious. Investors bought up stocks such as tech stocks and internet stocks. The sheer demand pushed up stock prices, which gave the appearance of genius to analysts' forecasts, yet the stock prices rose essentially as a self-fulfilling prophecy. The stocks were way overvalued and were cruisin' for a bruisin'. Analysts and investors were feeling lucky.

Investors, however, lost a ton of money (ooh, ugly). Money that people painstakingly accumulated over many years of work vanished in a matter of months as the bear market of 2000 hit (ooh, ugly). Of course, the bear market that hit in 2008–2009 was even more brutal. Retirees who had trusted the analysts saw nest eggs lose 40 percent to 70 percent in value (yikes, very ugly). Investors lost trillions during these major downturns, much of it needlessly. I'm sure lots of those folks thought they should've put that money in things that had enduring value instead — such as cookies and cases of merlot.

REMEMBER

During that bear market of 2000–2002, a record number of lawsuits and complaints were filed against brokerage firms. Wall Street and Main Street learned some tough lessons. Regarding research reports from brokerage firms, the following points can help you avoid getting a bad case of the uglies:

>> Always ask yourself, "Is the provider of the report a biased source?" In other words, is the broker getting business in any way from the company they're recommending?

>> Never, never, *never* rely on just one source of information, especially if it's the same source that's selling you the stock or other investment.

>> Do your research first before you rely on a brokerage report. Check out annual reports and the other documents I recommend earlier in this chapter.

>> Do your due diligence before you buy stocks anyway. Look at Parts 1 and 2 to understand your need for diversification, risk tolerance, and so on.

>> Verify the information provided to you with a trip to the library or websites.

Do It Yourself: Compiling Your Own Research Department

You don't need to spend an excessive amount of time or money, but you should maintain your own library of resources. You may need only one shelf (or a small amount of memory on your computer's hard drive), but why not have a few investment facts and resources at your fingertips? I maintain my own library loaded with books, magazines, newsletters, and tons of great stuff downloaded on my computer for easy search and reference. When you start your own collection, follow these tips:

>> **Keep some select newspapers.** *Barron's, The Wall Street Journal,* and *Investor's Business Daily* regularly have some editions that are worth keeping. For example, *The Wall Street Journal* and *Investor's Business Daily* usually publish a year-in-review issue the first business week in January. *Barron's* has special issues reviewing brokers and financial websites.

>> **Subscribe to financial magazines.** Publications such as *Forbes* and *Money* magazines offer great research and regularly review stocks, brokers, and resources for investors.

>> **Keep annual reports.** Regarding the stocks that are the core holdings in your portfolio, keep all the annual reports (at the very least, the most recent three).

>> **Go to the library's business reference section periodically to stay updated.** Hey, you pay the taxes that maintain the public library — you may as well use it to stay informed.

>> **Use the internet for research.** The web offers plenty of great sites to peruse.

TIP

Financial reports are very important and easier to read than most people think. An investor can easily avoid a bad investment by simply noticing the data in what seems like a jumble of numbers. Figure out how to read them. For a great book to help you with reading financial reports (without needless technicality), check out the latest edition of *How to Read a Financial Report: Wringing Vital Signs Out of the Numbers,* by John A. Tracy and Tage C. Tracy, or the latest edition of *Fundamental Analysis For Dummies,* by Matt Krantz (both published by Wiley).

IN THIS CHAPTER

» Finding out what brokers do

» Comparing full-service and discount brokers

» Selecting a broker

» Exploring the types of brokerage accounts

» Evaluating the recommendations of brokers

Chapter **8**

Working with Brokers

When you're ready to dive in and start investing in stocks, you first have to choose a broker. It's kind of like buying a car: You can do all the research in the world and know exactly what kind of car you want, but you still need a venue to conduct the actual transaction. Similarly, when you want to buy stock, your task is to do all the research you can to select the company you want to invest in. Still, you need a broker to actually buy the stock, whether you buy over the phone or online. In this chapter, I introduce you to the intricacies of the investor/broker relationship.

TIP

For information on various types of orders you can place with a broker, such as market orders, stop-loss orders, and so on, head to Chapter 13.

Defining the Broker's Role

The broker's primary role is to serve as the vehicle through which you either buy or sell stock. When I talk about brokers, I'm referring to companies such as Charles Schwab, TD Ameritrade, E*TRADE, and many other organizations that can buy stock on your behalf. Brokers can also be individuals who work for such firms. Although you can buy some stocks directly from the company that issues them, to purchase most stocks, you still need a brokerage account with a stockbroker.

REMEMBER

The distinction between institutional stockbrokers and personal stockbrokers is important:

>> **Institutional stockbrokers** make money from institutions and companies through investment banking and securities placement fees (such as initial public offerings [IPOs] and secondary offerings), advisory services, and other broker services.

>> **Personal stockbrokers** generally offer the same services to individuals and small businesses.

Although the primary task of brokers is the buying and selling of securities (the word *securities* refers to the world of financial or paper investments, and stocks are only a small part of that world), they can perform other tasks for you, including the following:

>> **Providing advisory services:** Investors pay brokers a fee for investment advice. Customers also get access to the firm's research.

>> **Offering limited banking services:** Brokers can offer features such as interest-bearing accounts, check writing, electronic deposits and withdrawals, and credit/debit cards.

>> **Brokering other securities:** In addition to stocks, brokers can buy bonds, mutual funds, options, exchange-traded funds (ETFs; see Chapter 11), and other investments on your behalf.

Personal stockbrokers make their money from individual investors like you and me through various fees, including the following:

>> **Brokerage commissions:** This fee is for buying and/or selling stocks and other securities. In recent times, some brokers have opted to greatly minimize or remove commissions.

>> **Margin interest charges:** This interest is charged to investors for borrowing against their brokerage account for investment purposes. (I discuss margin accounts in more detail later in this chapter.)

>> **Service charges:** These charges are for performing adminis-trative tasks and other functions. Brokers charge fees to investors for individual retirement accounts (IRAs) and for mailing stocks in certificate form.

Any broker (some brokers are now called *financial advisors*) you deal with should be registered with the Financial Industry Regulatory Authority (FINRA) and the Securities and Exchange Commission (SEC). In addition, to protect your money after you deposit it into a brokerage account, that broker should be a mem-ber of the Securities Investor Protection Corporation (SIPC). SIPC doesn't protect you from market losses; it protects your money in case the brokerage firm goes out of business or your losses are due to brokerage fraud. To find out whether the broker is registered with these organizations, contact FINRA (www.finra.org), SEC (www.sec.gov), or SIPC (www.sipc.org).

Comparing Full-Service and Discount Brokers

Stockbrokers fall into two basic categories, which I discuss in the following sections: full-service and discount. The type you choose really depends on what type of investor you are. Here are the dif-ferences in a nutshell:

>> **Full-service brokers** are suitable for investors who need some guidance and personal attention.

>> **Discount brokers** are better for those investors who are sufficiently confident and knowledgeable about stock investing to manage with minimal help (usually through the broker's website).

Before you deal with any broker (either full-service or discount), get a free report on the broker from FINRA by calling 800-289-9999 or through its website at www.finra.org. Through its service called BrokerCheck (https://brokercheck.finra.org), you can get a report on either a brokerage firm or an individual broker. You can find more details on this and other services (such as investor education and so forth) on FINRA's website. FINRA can tell you in its report whether any complaints or penalties have been filed against a brokerage firm or an individual rep.

At your disposal: Full-service brokers

Full-service brokers are just what the name indicates. They try to provide as many services as possible for investors who open accounts with them. When you open an account at a brokerage firm, a representative is assigned to your account. This representative is usually called an *account executive,* a *registered rep,* or a *financial advisor* by the brokerage firm. This person usually has a securities license (meaning that they're registered with FINRA and the SEC) and is knowledgeable about investing in general and stocks in particular.

Examples of full-service brokers are Goldman Sachs and Morgan Stanley. Of course, all brokers have full-featured websites to give you further information about their services. Get as informed as possible before you open your account. A full-service broker is there to help you build wealth, not make you, uh, broker.

What they can do for you

Your account executive is responsible for assisting you, answering questions about your account and the securities in your portfolio, and transacting your buy and sell orders. Here are some things that full-service brokers can do for you:

>> **Offer guidance and advice.** The greatest distinction between full-service brokers and discount brokers is the personal attention you receive from your account rep. You get to be on a first-name basis with a full-service broker, and you disclose a lot of information about your finances and financial goals. The rep is there to make recommendations about stocks and funds that may be suitable for you.

>> **Provide access to research.** Full-service brokers can give you access to their investment research department, which can give you in-depth information and analysis on a particular company. This information can be very valuable, but be aware of the pitfalls (see the later section "Judging Brokers' Recommendations").

>> **Help you achieve your investment objectives.** A good rep gets to know you and your investment goals and *then* offers advice and answers your questions about how specific investments and strategies can help you accomplish your wealth-building goals.

>> **Make investment decisions on your behalf.** Many investors don't want to be bothered when it comes to investment decisions. Full-service brokers can actually make decisions for your account with your authorization (this is also referred to as a *discretionary* account, although many brokers have scaled back the use of discretion for ordinary brokerage accounts). This service is fine, but be sure to require brokers to explain their choices to you.

What to watch out for

Although full-service brokers, with their seemingly limit-less assistance, can make life easy for an investor, you need to remember some important points to avoid problems:

>> **Brokers and account reps are salespeople.** No matter how well they treat you, they're still compensated based on their ability to produce revenue for the brokerage firm. They generate commissions and fees from you on behalf of the company. (In other words, they're paid to sell you things.)

REMEMBER

Whenever your rep makes a suggestion or recommendation, be sure to ask why and request a complete answer that includes the reasoning behind the recommendation. A good advisor is able to clearly explain the reasoning behind every suggestion. If you don't fully understand and agree with the advice, don't take it.

>> **Working with a full-service broker costs more than working with a discount broker.** Discount brokers are paid for simply buying or selling stocks for you. Full-service brokers do that and much more, like provide advice and guidance. Because of that, full-service brokers are more expensive (through higher brokerage commissions and advisory fees). Also, most full-service brokers expect you to invest at least $5,000 to $10,000 just to open an account, although many require higher minimums.

>> **Handing over decision-making authority to your rep can be a possible negative because letting others make financial decisions for you is always dicey — especially when they're using *your* money.** If they make poor investment choices that lose you money, you may not have any recourse because you authorized them to act on your behalf.

>> **Some brokers engage in an activity called** *churning.* Churning is basically buying and selling stocks for the sole purpose of generating commissions. Churning is great for brokers but bad for customers. If your account shows a lot of activity, ask for justification. Commissions, especially by full-service brokers, can take a big bite out of your wealth, so don't tolerate churning or other suspicious activity.

Just the basics: Discount brokers

Perhaps you don't need any hand-holding from a broker (that'd be kinda weird anyway). You know what you want, and you can make your own investment decisions. All you need is a convenient way to transact your buy and sell orders. In that case, go with a discount broker. They don't offer advice or premium services — just the basics required to perform your stock transactions.

Discount brokers, as the name implies, are cheaper to engage than full-service brokers. Because you're advising yourself (or getting advice and information from third parties such as newsletters, hotlines, or independent advisors), you can save on costs that you'd incur if you used a full-service broker.

If you choose to work with a discount broker, you must know as much as possible about your personal goals and needs. You have a greater responsibility for conducting adequate research to make good stock selections, and you must be prepared to accept the outcome, whatever that may be. (See the rest of Parts 2 and 3 for information you need before you get started.)

For a while, the regular investor had two types of discount brokers to choose from: conventional discount brokers and internet discount brokers. But the two are basically synonymous now, so the differences are hardly worth mentioning. Through industry consolidation, most of the conventional discount brokers today have full-featured websites, while internet discount brokers have adapted by adding more telephone and face-to-face services.

Charles Schwab (www.schwab.com) and Fidelity (www.fidelity.com) are examples of conventional discount brokers that have adapted well to the internet era. Internet brokers such as Ally (www.ally.com), E*TRADE (www.etrade.com), TradeStation (www.tradestation.com), and Webull (www.webull.com) have added more conventional services.

What they can do for you

Discount brokers offer some significant advantages over full-service brokers, such as the following:

>> **Lower cost:** This lower cost is usually the result of lower commissions (now to the point of no commissions), and it's the primary benefit of using discount brokers.

>> **Unbiased service:** Because they don't offer advice, discount brokers have no vested interest in trying to sell you any particular stock.

>> **Access to information:** Established discount brokers offer extensive educational materials on their websites.

>> **Extensive research:** Most brokers now offer their clients extensive research capabilities including stock and fund screening tools and access to comprehensive public company financial and trading data.

What to watch out for

Of course, doing business with discount brokers also has its downsides, including the following:

>> **No guidance:** Because you've chosen a discount broker, you *know* not to expect guidance, but the broker should make this fact clear to you anyway. If you're a knowledgeable investor, the lack of advice is considered a positive thing — no interference.

WARNING

>> **Hidden fees:** Discount brokers may shout about their lower commissions, but commissions aren't their only way of making money. Many discount brokers charge extra for services that you may think are included, such as issuing a stock certificate (rarely if ever done anymore) or mailing a statement. Ask whether they assess fees for maintaining IRAs or for transferring stocks and other securities (like bonds) in or out of your account, and find out what interest rates they charge for borrowing through brokerage accounts.

>> **Minimal customer service:** If you deal with an internet brokerage firm, find out about its customer service capability. If you can't transact business on its website, find out where you can call for assistance with your order.

Choosing a Broker

Before you choose a broker, you need to analyze your personal investing style (see Chapter 3), and then you can proceed to finding the kind of broker that fits your needs. It's almost like choosing shoes; if you don't know your size, you can't get a proper fit (and you can be in for a really uncomfortable future).

When it's time to choose a broker, keep the following points in mind:

REMEMBER

>> Match your investment style with a brokerage firm that charges the least amount of money for the services you're likely to use most frequently.

>> Compare all the costs of buying, selling, and holding stocks and other securities through a broker. Don't compare only commissions; compare other costs, too, like margin interest and other service charges (see the earlier section "Defining the Broker's Role" for more about these costs).

>> Use broker comparison services available in financial publications such as *Kiplinger's Personal Finance* and *Barron's* (and, of course, their websites), as well as online sources.

TIP

Finding brokers is easy. They're easily found online with your favorite search engine or on popular financial sites such as Investing.com (`www.investing.com`), Investopedia (`www.investopedia.com`), or MarketWatch (`www.marketwatch.com`). Many investment publishers — such as *Barron's* (`www.barrons.com`), Bloomberg (`www.bloomberg.com`), or *The Wall Street Journal* (`www.wsj.com`) — run comparisons on their sites.

Discovering Various Types of Brokerage Accounts

When you start investing in the stock market, you have to somehow actually *pay* for the stocks you buy. Most brokerage firms offer investors several types of accounts, each serving a different purpose. I present three of the most common types in the following sections. The basic difference boils down to how particular brokers view your creditworthiness when it comes to buying and selling securities. If your credit isn't great, your only choice is a cash account. If your credit is good, you can open either a cash account or a margin account. After you qualify for a margin account, you can (with additional approval) upgrade it to do options trades.

To open an account, you have to fill out an application and submit a check or money order for at least the minimum amount required to establish an account.

Cash accounts

A *cash account* (also referred to as a *Type 1 account*) means just what you'd think. You must deposit a sum of money along with the new account application to begin trading. The amount of your initial deposit varies from broker to broker. Some brokers have a minimum of $10,000; others let you open an account for as little as $500. Once in a while, you may see a broker offering cash accounts with no minimum deposit, usually as part of a promotion. Qualifying for a cash account is usually easy, as long as you have cash and a pulse.

With a cash account, your money has to be deposited in the account before the closing (or settlement) date for any trade you make. The closing occurs two business days after the date you make the trade (the *date of execution*). You may be required to have the money in the account even before the date of execution. (See Chapter 5 for details on these and other important dates.)

In other words, if you call your broker on Monday, October 10, and order 50 shares of CashLess Corp. at $20 per share, then on Wednesday, October 12, you'd better have $1,000 in cash sitting in your account (plus any additional cash needed to cover commissions if charged).

In addition, ask the broker how long it takes deposited cash (such as a check) to be available for investing. Some brokers put a hold on checks for up to ten business days (or longer, depending on the broker), regardless of how soon that check clears your account (that would drive me crazy!).

See whether your broker will pay you interest on the uninvested cash in your brokerage account. Some brokers offer a service in which uninvested money earns money-market rates, and you can even choose between a regular money-market account and a tax-free municipal money-market account.

Margin accounts

A *margin account* (also called a *Type 2 account*) gives you all the capabilities of a cash account plus allows you to borrow money against the securities in the account to buy more stock. Because you can borrow in a margin account, you have to be qualified and approved by the broker. After you're approved, this newfound credit gives you more leverage so you can buy more stock or do short selling. (You can read more about buying on margin and short selling in Chapter 13.)

For stock trading, the margin limit is 50 percent. For example, if you plan to buy $10,000 worth of stock on margin, you need at least $5,000 in cash (or securities owned) sitting in your account. The interest rate you pay varies depending on the broker, but most brokers generally charge a rate that's several points higher than their own borrowing rate.

Why use margin? Margin is to stocks what mortgage is to buying real estate. You can buy real estate with all cash, but using borrowed funds often makes sense because you may not have enough money to make a 100 percent cash purchase, or you may just prefer not to pay all cash. With margin, you can, for example, buy $10,000 worth of stock with as little as $5,000. The balance of the stock purchase is acquired using a loan (margin) from the brokerage firm.

WARNING

Personally, I'm not a big fan of margin, and I use it sparingly. Margin is a form of leverage that can work out fine if you're correct but can be very dangerous if the market moves against you. It's best applied with stocks that are generally stable and pay dividends. That way, the dividends help pay off the margin interest.

Options accounts

An *options account* (also referred to as a *Type 3 account*) gives you all the capabilities of a margin account plus the ability to trade options on stocks and stock indexes. To upgrade your margin account to an options account, the broker usually asks you to sign a statement that you're knowledgeable about options and familiar with the risks associated with them.

TIP

Options can be a very effective addition to a stock investor's array of wealth-building investment tools. A more comprehensive review of options is available in the book *Options Trading For Dummies*, by Joe Duarte (Wiley). I personally love to use options (as do my clients and students), and I think they can be a great tool in your wealth-building arsenal. That's why I provide extensive coverage of put and call options in my book *High-Level Investing For Dummies* (Wiley).

Judging Brokers' Recommendations

In recent years, Americans have become enamored with a new sport: the rating of stocks by brokers on TV financial shows. Frequently, these shows feature a dapper market strategist talking up a particular stock. Some stocks have been known to jump significantly right after an influential analyst issues a buy recommendation. Analysts' speculation and opinions make for great fun, and many people take their views very seriously. However, most investors should be very wary when analysts, especially the glib ones on TV, make a recommendation. It's often just showbiz. In the following sections, I define basic broker recommendations and list a few important considerations for evaluating them.

Understanding basic recommendations

Brokers issue their recommendations (advice) as a general idea of how much regard they have for a particular stock. The following list presents the basic recommendations (or ratings) and what they mean to you:

» **Strong buy and buy:** Hot diggity dog! These ratings are the ones to get. The analyst loves this pick, and you would be very wise to get a bunch of shares. The thing to keep in mind, however, is that buy recommendations are probably the most common because — let's face it — brokers sell stocks.

» **Accumulate and market perform:** An analyst who issues these types of recommendations is positive, yet unexcited, about the pick. This rating is akin to asking a friend whether they like your new suit and getting the response "It's nice" in a monotone voice. It's a polite reply, but you wish their opinion had been more definitive. For some brokers, accumulate is considered a buy recommendation.

» **Hold or neutral:** Analysts use this language when their backs are to the wall, but they still don't want to say, "Sell that loser!" This recommendation reminds me of my mother telling me to be nice and either say something positive or keep my mouth shut. In this case, the rating is the analyst's way of keeping their mouth shut.

>> **Sell:** Many analysts should've issued this recommendation during the bear markets of 2000–2002 and 2008 but didn't. What a shame. So many investors lost money because some analysts were too nice (or biased?) or afraid to be honest, sound the alarm, and urge people to sell.

>> **Avoid like the plague:** I'm just kidding about this one, but I wish this recommendation were available. I've seen plenty of stocks that I thought were dreadful investments — stocks of companies that made no money, were in terrible financial condition, and should never have been considered at all. Yet investors gobble up billions of dollars' worth of stocks that eventually become worthless.

Asking a few important questions

Don't get me wrong. An analyst's recommendation is certainly a better tip than what you'd get from your barber or your sister-in-law's neighbor, but you want to view recommendations from analysts with a healthy dose of reality. Analysts have biases because their employment depends on the very companies that are being presented. What investors need to listen to when a broker talks up a stock is the reasoning *behind* the recommendation. In other words, *why* is the broker making this recommendation?

Keep in mind that analysts' recommendations can play a useful role in your personal stock-investing research. If you find a great stock and *then* you hear analysts give glowing reports on the same stock, you're on the right track! Here are some questions to keep in mind:

>> **How does the analyst arrive at a rating?** The analyst's approach to evaluating a stock can help you round out your research as you consult other sources such as newsletters and independent advisory services.

>> **What analytical approach is the analyst using?** Some analysts use *fundamental analysis* (see Chapters 6 and 9) — looking at the company's financial condition and factors related to its success, such as its standing within the industry

and the overall market. Other analysts use *technical analysis* — looking at the company's stock price history and judging past stock price movements to derive some insight regarding the stock's future price movement. Many analysts use a combination of the two. Is this analyst's approach similar to your approach or to those of sources that you respect or admire?

>> **What is the analyst's track record?** Has the analyst had a consistently good record through both bull and bear markets? Major financial publications, such as *Barron's* and *Hulbert Financial Digest,* and websites, such as MarketWatch (www.marketwatch.com), regularly track recommendations from well-known analysts and stock pickers.

>> **How does the analyst treat important aspects of the company's performance, such as sales and earnings?** How about the company's balance sheet? The essence of a healthy company is growing sales and earnings coupled with strong assets and low debt. (See Chapter 6 for more details on these topics.)

>> **Is the industry that the company's in doing well?** Do the analysts give you insight on this important information? A strong company in a weak industry can't stay strong for long. The right industry is a critical part of the stock-selection process (for more information, see Chapter 12).

>> **What research sources does the analyst cite?** Does the analyst quote the federal government or industry trade groups to support their thesis? These sources are important because they help give a more complete picture regarding the company's prospects for success. Imagine that you decide on the stock of a strong company. What if the federal government (through agencies like the SEC) is penalizing the company for fraudulent activity? Or what if the company's industry is shrinking or has ceased to grow (making it tougher for the company to continue growing)? The astute investor looks at a variety of sources before buying stock.

>> **Is the analyst rational when citing a target price for a stock?** When the analyst says, "We think this $40 stock will hit $100 per share within 12 months," are they presenting a rational model, such as basing the share price on a projected price-to-earnings ratio (see Chapter 6)? The analyst must be able to provide a logical scenario explaining why the stock has a good chance of achieving the cited target price within

the time frame mentioned. You may not necessarily agree with the analyst's conclusion, but the explanation can help you decide whether the stock choice is well thought out.

WARNING

>> **Does the analyst or the analyst's firm have any ties to the company they're recommending?** During 2000–2002, the financial industry got bad publicity because many analysts gave positive recommendations on stocks of companies that were doing business with the very firms that employed those analysts. This conflict of interest is probably the biggest reason that analysts were so wrong in their recommendations during that period. Ask your broker to disclose any conflict of interest. Additionally, brokers are required to disclose whether their firm is involved with a particular stock as a *market maker* (acting as an investment banker and bringing IPOs for sale to investors) or in another capacity (such as being its investment banker).

>> **What school of economic thought does the analyst adhere to?** This may sound like an odd question, and it may not be readily answered, but it's a good thing to know. If I had to choose between two analysts who were very similar except that Analyst A adhered to the Keynesian school of economic thought, and Analyst B adhered to the Austrian school, guess what? I'd choose Analyst B because those who embrace the Austrian school have a much better grasp of real-world economics (which means better stock-investment choices).

REMEMBER

The bottom line with brokerage recommendations is that you shouldn't use them to buy or sell a stock. Instead, use them to confirm your own research. I know that if I buy a stock based on my own research and later discover the same stock being talked up on the financial shows, that's just the icing on the cake. The experts may be great to listen to, and their recommendations can augment your own opinions, but they're no substitute for your own careful research. Parts 2 and 3 of this book (including this chapter) help you lay the groundwork for your stock-investing strategy.

3

Understanding Essential Stock Strategies and Tactics

Investigate the key elements of a great growth stock.

Find out how to gain cash flow by choosing a solid dividend-income stock and writing covered calls.

Invest in the best stocks with a single exchange-traded fund (ETF) purchase.

Check out the hottest sectors that will be growing in the coming years.

Discover how brokerage orders can help you maximize profits and minimize losses (even in bear markets).

Find out how you can keep the tax bite on your profits to a minimum.

Chapter **9**

Investing in Stocks for Long-Term Growth

W hat's the number-one reason people invest in stocks? To grow their wealth (also referred to as *capital appreciation*). Yes, some people invest for income (in the form of dividends), but that's a different matter (see Chapter 10). Investors seeking growth would rather see the money that could've been distributed as dividends be reinvested in the company so that (hopefully) a greater gain will be achieved when the stock's price rises or appreciates. People interested in growing their wealth see stocks as one of the convenient ways to do it. Growth stocks tend to be riskier than other categories of stocks, but they offer excellent long-term prospects for making the big bucks. If you don't believe me, just ask Warren Buffett, Peter Lynch, and other successful, long-term investors.

Although someone like Buffett is not considered a growth investor, his long-term, value-oriented approach has been a successful growth strategy. If you're the type of investor who has enough time to let somewhat risky stocks trend upward or who has enough money so that a loss won't devastate you financially, then growth stocks are definitely for you. As they say, no guts, no glory. The challenge is to figure out which stocks make you richer quicker; I give you tips on how to do so in this chapter.

Short of starting your own business, stock investing is the best way to profit from a business venture. I want to emphasize that to make money in stocks consistently over the long haul, you must remember that you're investing in a *company*; buying the stock is just a means for you to participate in the company's success (or failure). Why does it matter that you think of stock investing as buying a *company* versus buying a *stock?* Invest in a stock only if you're just as excited about it as you would be if you were the CEO in charge of running the company. If you're the sole owner of the company, do you act differently than one of a legion of obscure stockholders? Of course you do. As the firm's owner, you have a greater interest in the company. You have a strong desire to know how the enterprise is doing. As you invest in stocks, make believe that you're the owner, and take an active interest in the company's products, services, sales, earnings, and so on. This attitude and discipline can enhance your goals as a stock investor. This approach is especially important if your investment goal is growth.

Becoming a Value-Oriented Growth Investor

A stock is considered a *growth stock* when it's growing faster and at a higher rate than the overall stock market. Basically, a growth stock performs better than its peers in categories such as sales and earnings. *Value stocks* are stocks that are priced lower than the value of the company and its assets — you can identify a value stock by analyzing the company's fundamentals and looking at key financial ratios, such as the price-to-earnings (P/E) ratio. (I cover company finances and ratios in Chapter 6.) Growth stocks tend to have better prospects for growth in the immediate future (from one to four years), but value stocks tend to have less risk and steadier growth over a longer term.

Over the years, a debate has quietly raged in the financial community about growth versus value investing. Some people believe that growth and value are mutually exclusive. They maintain that large numbers of people buying stock with growth as the expectation tend to drive up the stock price relative to the company's current value. Growth investors, for example, aren't put off by P/E ratios of 30, 40, or higher. Value investors, meanwhile, are too nervous to buy stocks at those P/E ratio levels.

However, you *can* have both. A value-oriented approach to growth investing serves you best. Long-term growth stock investors spend time analyzing the company's fundamentals to make sure that the company's growth prospects lie on a solid foundation. But what if you have to choose between a growth stock and a value stock? Which do you choose? Seek value when you're buying the stock and analyze the company's prospects for growth. Growth includes, but is not limited to, the health and growth of the company's specific industry, the economy at large, and the general political climate (see Chapter 12).

REMEMBER

The bottom line is that growth is much easier to achieve when you seek solid, value-oriented companies in growing industries. (To better understand industries and sectors and how they affect stock value, see Chapter 12.) It's also worth emphasizing that time, patience, and discipline are key factors in your success — especially in the tumultuous and uncertain stock-investing environment of the current time.

TECHNICAL
STUFF

Value-oriented growth investing probably has the longest history of success compared to most stock-investing philosophies. The track record for those people who use value-oriented growth investing is enviable. Warren Buffett, Benjamin Graham, John Templeton, and Peter Lynch are a few of the more well-known practitioners. Each may have his own spin on the concepts, but all have successfully applied the basic principles of value-oriented growth investing over many years.

Choosing Growth Stocks with a Few Handy Tips

Although the information in the previous section can help you shrink your stock choices from thousands of stocks to maybe a few dozen or a few hundred (depending on how well the general stock market is doing), the purpose of this section is to help you cull the so-so growth stocks to unearth the go-go ones. It's time to dig deeper for the biggest potential winners. Keep in mind that you probably won't find a stock to satisfy all the criteria presented here. Just make sure that your selection meets as many criteria as realistically possible. But hey, if you do find a stock that meets all the criteria cited, *buy as much as you can!*

Verifiably, 80 percent to 90 percent of my stock picks are profitable. People ask me how I pick a winning stock. I tell them that I don't just pick a stock and hope that it does well. In fact, my personal stock-picking research doesn't even begin with stocks; I first look at the investing environment (politics, economics, demographics, and so on) and choose which industry will benefit. After I know which industry will prosper accordingly, *then* I start to analyze and choose my stock(s).

After I choose a stock, I wait. Patience is more than just a virtue; patience is to investing what time is to a seed that's planted in fertile soil. The legendary Jesse Livermore said that he didn't make his stock-market fortunes by trading stocks; his fortunes were made "in the waiting." Why?

When I tell you to have patience and a long-term perspective, it isn't because I want you to wait years or decades for your stock portfolio to bear fruit. It's because you're waiting for a specific condition to occur: for the market to discover what you have! When you have a good stock in a good industry, it takes time for the market to discover it. When a stock has more buyers than sellers, it rises — it's as simple as that. As time passes, more buyers find your stock. As the stock rises, it attracts more attention and, therefore, more buyers. The more time that passes, the better your stock looks to the investing public.

REMEMBER

When you're choosing growth stocks, you should consider investing in a company only *if* it makes a profit and *if* you understand *how* it makes that profit and from *where* it generates sales. Part of your research means looking at the industry and sector (see Chapter 12) and economic trends in general.

Looking for leaders in megatrends

A strong company in a growing industry is a common recipe for success. If you look at the history of stock investing, this point comes up constantly. Investors need to be on the alert for megatrends because they help ensure success.

A *megatrend* is a major development that has huge implications for much (if not all) of society for a long time to come. Good examples are the advent of the internet and the aging of America. Both of these trends offer significant challenges and opportunities for the economy. Take the internet, for example. Its potential for economic application is still being developed. Millions are flocking to it for many reasons. And census data tells us that senior citizens (those over 65) will continue to be a fast-growing segment of the U.S. population during the next 20 years. (Millennials are another huge demographic that investors should be aware of.) How does the stock investor take advantage of a megatrend? Find out more in Chapter 12.

Comparing the growth of a company versus an industry

You have to measure the growth of a company against something to figure out whether its stock is a growth stock. Usually, you compare the growth of a company with growth from other companies in the same industry or with the stock market in general. In practical terms, when you measure the growth of a stock against the stock market, you're actually comparing it against a generally accepted benchmark, such as the Dow Jones Industrial Average (DJIA) or the Standard & Poor's 500 (S&P 500). For more on stock indexes, see Chapter 11.

TIP

If a company's earnings grow 15 percent per year over three years or more, and the industry's average growth rate over the same time frame is 10 percent, then the stock qualifies as a growth stock. You can easily calculate the earnings growth rate by comparing a company's earnings in the current year to the preceding year and computing the difference as a percentage. For example, if a company's earnings (on a per-share basis) were $1 last year and $1.10 this year, then earnings grew by 10 percent. Many analysts also look at a current quarter and compare the earnings to the same quarter from the preceding year to see whether earnings are growing.

REMEMBER

A growth stock is called that not only because the company is growing but also because the company is performing well with some consistency. Having a single year where your earnings do well versus the S&P 500's average doesn't cut it. Growth must be consistently accomplished.

Considering a company with a strong niche

Companies that have established a strong niche are consistently profitable. Look for a company with one or more of the following characteristics:

>> **A strong brand:** Companies such as Coca-Cola and Microsoft come to mind. Yes, other companies out there can make soda or software, but a business needs a lot more than a similar product to topple companies that have established an almost irrevocable identity with the public.

>> **High barriers to entry:** UPS and FedEx have set up tremendous distribution and delivery networks that competitors can't easily duplicate. High barriers to entry offer an important edge to companies that are already established. Examples of high barriers include high capital requirements (needing lots of cash to start) or special technology that's not easily produced or acquired.

>> **Research and development (R&D):** Companies such as Pfizer and Merck spend a lot of money researching and developing new pharmaceutical products. This investment becomes a new product with millions of consumers who become loyal purchasers, so the company's going to grow. You can find out what companies spend on R&D by checking their financial statements and their annual reports (more on this in Chapters 6 and 7).

Checking out a company's fundamentals

When you hear the word *fundamentals* in the world of stock investing, it refers to the company's financial condition, operating performance, and related data. When investors (especially value investors) do *fundamental analysis*, they look at the company's fundamentals — its balance sheet, income statement, cash flow, and other operational data, along with external factors such as the company's market position, industry, and economic prospects. Essentially, the fundamentals indicate the company's financial condition. Chapter 6 goes into greater detail about analyzing a company's financial condition. However, the main numbers you want to look at include the following:

>> **Sales:** Are the company's sales this year surpassing last year's? As a decent benchmark, you want to see sales at least 10 percent higher than last year. Although it may differ depending on the industry, 10 percent is a reasonable, general yardstick.

>> **Earnings:** Are earnings at least 10 percent higher than last year? Earnings should grow at the same rate as sales (or, hopefully, better).

>> **Debt:** Is the company's total debt equal to or lower than the prior year? The death knell of many a company has been excessive debt.

TIP

A company's financial condition has more factors than I mention here, but these numbers are the most important. I also realize that using the 10 percent figure may seem like an oversimplification, but you don't need to complicate matters unnecessarily. I know someone's computerized financial model may come out to 9.675 percent or maybe 11.07 percent, but keep it simple for now.

Evaluating a company's management

The management of a company is crucial to its success. Before you buy stock in a company, you want to know that the company's management is doing a great job. But how do you do that? If you call up a company and ask, it may not even return your phone call. How do you know whether management is running the company properly? The best way is to check the numbers. The following sections tell you the numbers you need to check. If the company's management is running the business well, the ultimate result is a rising stock price.

Return on equity

REMEMBER

Although you can measure how well management is doing in several ways, you can take a quick snapshot of a management team's competence by checking the company's return on equity (ROE). You calculate the ROE simply by dividing earnings by equity. The resulting percentage gives you a good idea whether the company is using its equity (or net assets) efficiently and profitably. Basically, the higher the percentage, the better, but you can consider the ROE solid if the percentage is 10 percent or higher. Keep in mind that not all industries have identical ROEs.

To find out a company's earnings, check out the company's income statement. The *income statement* is a simple financial statement that expresses this equation:

Sales (or revenue) – Expenses = Net earnings (or net income or net profit)

You can see an example of an income statement in Table 9-1. (I give more details on income statements in Chapter 6.)

TABLE 9-1 Grobaby, Inc., Income Statement

	2021 Income Statement	2022 Income Statement
Sales	$82,000	$90,000
Expenses	–$75,000	–$78,000
Net earnings	$7,000	$12,000

To find out a company's equity, check out that company's balance sheet. (See Chapter 6 for more details on balance sheets.) The *balance sheet* is actually a simple financial statement that illustrates this equation:

Total assets – Total liabilities = Net equity

For public stock companies, the net assets are called *shareholders' equity* or simply *equity.* Table 9-2 shows a balance sheet for Grobaby, Inc.

TABLE 9-2 Grobaby, Inc., Balance Sheet

	Balance Sheet as of December 31, 2021	Balance Sheet as of December 31, 2022
Total assets (TA)	$55,000	$65,000
Total liabilities (TL)	–$20,000	–$25,000
Equity (TA – TL)	$35,000	$40,000

Table 9-1 shows that Grobaby's earnings went from $7,000 to $12,000. In Table 9-2, you can see that Grobaby increased the equity from $35,000 to $40,000 in one year. The ROE for the year 2021 is 20 percent ($7,000 in earnings ÷ $35,000 in equity), which is a solid number. The following year, the ROE is 30 percent ($12,000 in earnings ÷ $40,000 in equity), another solid number. A good minimum ROE is 10 percent, but 15 percent or more is preferred.

Equity and earnings growth

Two additional barometers of success are a company's growth in earnings and growth of equity:

>> Look at the growth in earnings in Table 9-1. The earnings grew from $7,000 (in 2021) to $12,000 (in 2022), a percentage increase of 71 percent ($12,000 – $7,000 = $5,000, and $5,000 ÷ $7,000 = 71 percent), which is excellent. At a minimum, earnings growth should be equal to or better than the rate of inflation, but because that's not always a reliable number, I like at least 10 percent.

>> In Table 9-2, Grobaby's equity grew by $5,000 (from $35,000 to $40,000), or 14.3 percent ($5,000 ÷ $35,000), which is very good — management is doing good things here. I like to see equity increasing by 10 percent or more.

Insider buying

TIP

Watching management as it manages the business is important, but another indicator of how well the company is doing is to see whether management is buying stock in the company as well. If a company is poised for growth, who knows better than management? And if management is buying up the company's stock en masse, that's a great indicator of the stock's potential.

Noticing who's buying and/ or recommending a stock

You can invest in a great company and still see its stock go nowhere. Why? Because what makes the stock go up is demand — when there's more buying than selling of the stock. If you pick a stock for all the right reasons and the market notices the stock as well, that attention causes the stock price to climb. The things to watch for include the following:

>> **Institutional buying:** Are mutual funds and pension plans buying up the stock you're looking at? If so, this type of buying power can exert tremendous upward pressure on the stock's price. Some resources and publications track institutional buying and how that affects any particular stock. Frequently, when a mutual fund buys a stock, others soon follow. In spite of all the talk about independent research, a herd mentality still exists.

>> **Analysts' attention:** Are analysts talking about the stock on the financial shows? As much as you should be skeptical about an analyst's recommendation (given the stock market debacle of 2000–2002, the market crisis of 2008, and the bear market of 2022), it offers some positive reinforcement for your stock. Don't ever buy a stock solely on the basis of an analyst's recommendation. Just know that if you buy a stock based on your own research, and analysts subsequently rave about it, your stock price is likely to go up. A single recommendation by an influential analyst can be enough to send a stock skyward.

>> **Newsletter recommendations:** Independent researchers usually publish newsletters. If influential newsletters are touting your choice, that praise is also good for your stock. Although some great newsletters are out there and they offer information that's as good as or better than that of some brokerage firms' research departments, don't base your investment decision on a single tip. However, seeing newsletters tout a stock that you've already chosen should make you feel good.

>> **Consumer publications:** No, you won't find investment advice here. This one seems to come out of left field, but it's a source that you should notice. Publications such as *Consumer Reports* regularly look at products and services and rate them for consumer satisfaction. If a company's offerings are well received by consumers, that's a strong positive for the company. This kind of attention ultimately has a positive effect on that company's stock.

Making sure a company continues to do well

A company's financial situation does change, and you, as a diligent investor, need to continue to look at the numbers for as long as the stock is in your portfolio. You may have chosen a great stock from a great company with great numbers in 2018, but chances are pretty good that the numbers have changed since then.

WARNING

Great stocks don't always stay that way. A great selection that you're drawn to today may become tomorrow's pariah. Information, both good and bad, moves like lightning. Keep an eye on your stock company's numbers! For more information on a company's financial data, check out Chapter 6.

Heeding investing lessons from history

A growth stock isn't a creature like the Loch Ness monster — always talked about but rarely seen. Growth stocks have been part of the financial scene for nearly a century. Examples abound that offer rich information that you can apply to today's stock-market environment. Look at past market winners, especially those during the bull market of the late 1990s and the bearish markets of 2000–2010, and ask yourself, "What made them profitable stocks?" I mention these two time frames because they offer a stark contrast to each other. The 1990s were booming times for stocks, whereas more recent years were very tough and bearish.

REMEMBER

Being aware and acting logically are as vital to successful stock investing as they are to any other pursuit. Over and over again, history gives you the formula for successful stock investing:

>> Pick a company that has strong fundamentals, including signs such as rising sales and earnings and low debt (see Chapter 6).

>> Make sure that the company is in a growing industry (see Chapter 12).

>> Fully participate in stocks that are benefiting from bullish market developments in the general economy.

>> During a bear market or in bearish trends, switch more of your money out of growth stocks (such as technology) and into defensive stocks (such as utilities).

>> Monitor your stocks. Hold onto stocks that continue to have growth potential, and sell those stocks with declining prospects.

Chapter **10**
Investing in Stocks for Income and Cash Flow

Stocks are well known for their ability to appreciate (for capital gains potential), but not enough credit is given regarding stocks' ability to boost your income and cash flow. Given that income will be a primary concern for many in the coming months and years (especially baby boomers and others concerned with retirement, pension issues, and so on), I consider this to be an important chapter.

The first income feature is the obvious — dividends! I love dividends, and they have excellent features that make them very attractive, such as their ability to meet or exceed the rate of inflation and the fact that they're subject to lower taxes than, say, regular taxable interest or wages. Dividend-paying stocks (also called *income stocks*) deserve a spot in a variety of portfolios, especially those of investors at or near retirement. Also, I think that younger folks (such as millennials) can gain long-term financial benefits from having dividends reinvested to compound their growth (such as with dividend reinvestment plans). In this chapter, I show you how to analyze income stocks with a few handy formulas, and I describe several typical income stocks.

Dividends are the primary subject here, but I cover much more. Many stocks in your portfolio give you the firepower to generate substantial income from call and put options (sweet!). Income from options (and other income strategies) come later in this chapter, but I get to dividends first.

Understanding the Basics of Income Stocks

I certainly think that dividend-paying stocks are a great consideration for those investors seeking greater income in their portfolios. I especially like stocks with higher-than-average dividends that are known as *income stocks*. Income stocks take on a dual role: Not only can they appreciate, but they can also provide regular income. The following sections take a closer look at dividends and income stocks.

Getting a grip on dividends and dividend rates

When people talk about gaining income from stocks, they're usually talking about dividends. Dividends are pro rata distributions that treat every stockholder the same. A *dividend* is nothing more than pro rata periodic distributions of cash (or sometimes stock) to the stock owner. You purchase dividend stocks primarily for income — not for spectacular growth potential.

Dividends are sometimes confused with interest. However, dividends are payouts to owners, whereas *interest* is a payment to a creditor. A stock investor is considered a part owner of the company they invest in and is entitled to dividends when they're issued. A bank, on the other hand, considers you a creditor when you open an account; the bank borrows your money and pays you interest on it.

A dividend is quoted as an annual dollar amount (or percentage yield), but it's usually paid on a quarterly basis. For example, if a stock pays a dividend of $4 per share, you're probably paid $1 every quarter. If, in this example, you have 200 shares, you're paid $800 every year (if the dividend doesn't change during that period), or $200 per quarter. Getting that regular dividend check every three months (for as long as you hold the stock) can be a nice perk. If the company continues to do well, that dividend can grow over time. A good income stock has a higher-than-average dividend (typically, 4 percent or higher).

REMEMBER

Dividend rates aren't guaranteed, and they're subject to the decisions of the stock issuer's board of directors — they can go up or down, or in some extreme cases, the dividend can be suspended or even discontinued. Fortunately, most companies that issue dividends continue them indefinitely and actually increase dividend payments from time to time. Historically, dividend increases have equaled (or exceeded) the rate of inflation.

Recognizing who's well suited for income stocks

What type of person is best suited to income stocks? Income stocks can be appropriate for many investors, but they're an especially good match for the following individuals:

>> **Conservative and novice investors:** Conservative investors like to see a slow but steady approach to growing their money while getting regular dividend checks. Novice investors who want to start slowly also benefit from income stocks.

>> **Retirees:** Growth investing (see Chapter 9) is best suited for long-term needs, whereas income investing is best suited to current needs. Retirees may want some growth in their portfolios, but they're more concerned with regular income that can keep pace with inflation.

>> **Dividend reinvestment plan (DRP) investors:** For those investors who like to compound their money with DRPs, income stocks are perfect.

TIP

Given recent economic trends and conditions for the foreseeable future, I think that dividends should be a mandatory part of the stock investor's wealth-building approach. This is especially true for those in or approaching retirement. Investing in stocks that have a reliable track record of increasing dividends is now easier than ever. In fact, there are exchange-traded funds (ETFs) that are focused on stocks with a long and consistent track record of raising dividends (typically on an annual basis). Such ETFs can be found at sites such as https://etfdb.com — use search terms such as "high dividend," "dividend growth," or "dividend yield" to find them. (You can find more about ETFs in Chapter 11.)

Assessing the advantages of income stocks

Income stocks tend to be among the least volatile of all stocks, and many investors view them as defensive stocks. *Defensive stocks* are stocks of companies that sell goods and services that are generally needed no matter what shape the economy is in. (Don't confuse defensive stocks with *defense stocks*, which specialize in goods and equipment for the military.) Food, beverage, and utility companies are great examples of defensive stocks. Even when the economy is experiencing tough times, people still need to eat, drink, and turn on the lights. Companies that offer relatively high dividends also tend to be large firms in established, stable industries.

TIP

Some industries in particular are known for high-dividend stocks. Utilities (such as electric, gas, and water), real estate investment trusts (REITs), and the energy sector (oil and gas royalty trusts) are places where you definitely find income stocks. Yes, you can find high-dividend stocks in other industries, but you find a higher concentration of them in these industries. For more details, see the sections highlighting these industries later in this chapter.

Heeding the disadvantages of income stocks

Before you say, "Income stocks are great! I'll get my checkbook and buy a batch right now," take a look at the following potential disadvantages (ugh!). Income stocks do come with some fine print.

What goes up . . .

Income stocks can go down as well as up, just as any stock can. The factors that affect stocks in general — politics, megatrends (see Chapter 12), different kinds of risk (see Chapter 4), and so on — affect income stocks, too. Fortunately, income stocks don't get hit as hard as other stocks when the market is declining because high dividends tend to act as a support to the stock price.

Therefore, income stocks' prices usually fall less dramatically than other stocks' prices in a declining market.

Interest-rate sensitivity

Income stocks can be sensitive to rising interest rates. When interest rates go up, other investments (such as corporate bonds, U.S. Treasury securities, and bank certificates of deposit [CDs]) are more attractive. When your income stock yields 4 percent and interest rates go up to 5 percent, 6 percent, or higher, you may think, "Hmm, why settle for a 4 percent yield when I can get better elsewhere?" As more and more investors sell their low-yield stocks, the prices for those stocks fall.

Another point to note is that rising interest rates may hurt the company's financial strength. If the company has to pay more interest, that may affect the company's earnings, which, in turn, may affect the company's ability to continue paying dividends.

REMEMBER

Dividend-paying companies that experience consistently falling revenues tend to cut dividends. In this case, *consistent* means two or more years.

The effect of inflation

Although many companies raise their dividends on a regular basis, some don't. Or if they do raise their dividends, the increases may be small. If income is your primary consideration, you want to be aware of this fact. If you're getting the same dividend year after year and this income is important to you, rising inflation becomes a problem.

Say that you have XYZ stock at $10 per share with an indicated annual dividend of 30 cents. The yield is 3 percent (30 cents ÷ $10). If you have a yield of 3 percent two years in a row, how do you feel when inflation rises 6 percent one year and 7 percent the next year? Because inflation means your costs are rising, inflation shrinks the value of the dividend income you receive.

Fortunately, studies show that, in general, dividends do better in inflationary environments than bonds and other fixed-rate investments do. Usually, the dividends of companies that provide consumer staples (food, energy, and so on) meet or exceed the rate of inflation. This is why some investment gurus describe companies that pay growing dividends as having stocks that are "better than bonds."

STOCK DIVIDENDS — OR COMPANY DIVIDENDS?

The term *stock dividend* is commonly used in financial discussions about the stock market. However, the reality is that dividends are not paid by stocks; they're paid pro rata distributions of cash by companies. It may sound like I'm splitting hairs, but it's a fundamental difference. Stock prices are subject to the whims of market buying and selling — one day the share prices are up nicely; the next day prices go down when that day's headlines spook the market. Because the dividend isn't volatile and it's paid with regularity (quarterly usually), it's more predictable. I think that investors should be in the business of "collecting cash flows" as opposed to fretting over the ebbs and flows of the market.

What does that mean? If a hundred shares of a given dividend-paying stock provide, say, $100 per year in annual dividends, the income-minded stock investor should keep a running tally of annual dividend amounts. That way, they keep investing until they reach a desired income level (such as $2,000 annual dividend income) and feel confident that this dividend income can be relatively reliable and will keep growing as payouts grow from company operations. Lastly, keep in mind that technically a "stock dividend" is actually a pro rata distribution of stock (and not cash).

Uncle Sam's cut

The government usually taxes dividends as ordinary income. Find out from your tax person whether potentially higher tax rates on dividends are in effect for the current or subsequent tax year. (See Chapter 14 for more information on taxes for stock investors.)

Analyzing Income Stocks

As I explain in the preceding section, even conservative income investors can be confronted with different types of risk. (Chapter 4 covers risk and volatility in greater detail.) Fortunately, this section helps you carefully choose income stocks so you can minimize potential disadvantages.

TIP

Look at income stocks in the same way you do growth stocks when assessing the financial strength of a company. Getting nice dividends comes to a screeching halt if the company can't afford to pay them. If your budget depends on dividend income, then monitoring the company's financial strength is that much more important. You can apply the same techniques I list in Chapters 6 and 9 for assessing the financial strength of growth stocks to your assessment of income stocks.

Pinpointing your needs first

You choose income stocks primarily because you want or need income now. As a secondary point, income stocks have the potential for steady, long-term appreciation. So, if you're investing for retirement needs that won't occur for another 20 years, maybe income stocks aren't suitable for you — a better choice may be to invest in growth stocks because they're more likely to grow your money faster over a lengthier investment term. (I explain who's best suited to income stocks earlier in this chapter.)

If you're certain you want income stocks, do a rough calculation to figure out how big a portion of your portfolio you want income stocks to occupy. Suppose you need $25,000 in investment income to satisfy your current financial needs. If you have bonds that give you $20,000 in interest income, and you want the rest to come from dividends from income stocks, you need to choose stocks that pay you $5,000 in annual dividends. If you have $100,000 left to invest, you need a portfolio of income stocks that yields 5 percent ($5,000 ÷ $100,000 = 5 percent; I explain yield in more detail in the following section).

You may ask, "Why not just buy $100,000 of bonds (for instance) that may yield at least 5 percent?" Well, if you're satisfied with that $5,000, and inflation for the foreseeable future is 0 or considerably less than 5 percent, then you have a point. Unfortunately, inflation (low or otherwise) will probably be with us for a long time. Fortunately, the steady growth of the dividends that income stocks provide is a benefit to you.

TIP

If you have income stocks and don't have any immediate need for the dividends, consider reinvesting the dividends in the company's stock.

Every investor is different. If you're not sure about your current or future needs, your best bet is to consult with a financial planner.

Checking out yield

Because income stocks pay out dividends — income — you need to assess which stocks can give you the highest income. How do you do that? The main thing to look for is *yield*, which is the percentage rate of return paid on a stock in the form of dividends. Looking at a stock's dividend yield is the quickest way to find out how much money you'll earn with this stock compared to other dividend-paying stocks (or even other investments, such as a bank account). Table 10-1 illustrates this point. Dividend yield is calculated in the following way:

Dividend yield = Dividend income ÷ Stock investment

TABLE 10-1 Comparing Yields

Investment	Type	Investment Amount	Annual Investment Income (Dividend)	Yield (Annual Investment Income Divided by Investment Amount)
Smith Co.	Common stock	$20 per share	$1 per share	5%
Jones Co.	Common stock	$30 per share	$1.50 per share	5%
Wilson Bank	Savings account	$1,000 deposit	$10 (interest)	1%

The next two sections use the information in Table 10-1 to compare the yields from different investments and to show how evaluating yield helps you choose the stock that earns you the most money.

Don't stop scrutinizing stocks after you acquire them. You may make a great choice that gives you a great dividend, but that doesn't mean the stock will continue to perform indefinitely. Monitor the company's progress for as long as the stock is in your portfolio by using resources such as www.bloomberg.com and www.marketwatch.com.

Examining changes in yield

Most people have no problem understanding yield when it comes to bank accounts. If I tell you that my bank CD has an annual yield of 3.5 percent, you can easily figure out that if I deposit $1,000 in that account, a year later I'll have $1,035 (slightly more if you include compounding). The CD's market value in this example is the same as the deposit amount — $1,000. That makes it easy to calculate.

REMEMBER

How about stocks? When you see a stock listed in the financial pages, the dividend yield is provided, along with the stock's price and annual dividend. The dividend yield in the financial pages is always calculated based on the closing price of the stock on that given day. Just keep in mind that based on supply and demand, stock prices will fluctuate throughout trading hours, so the yield changes throughout trading hours, too. So, keep the following two things in mind when examining yield:

>> **The yield listed in the financial pages may not represent the yield you're receiving.** What if you bought stock in Smith Co. (refer to Table 10-1) a month ago at $20 per share? With an annual dividend of $1, you know your yield is 5 percent. But what if today Smith Co. is selling for $40 per share? If you look in the financial pages, the yield quoted is 2.5 percent. Gasp! Did the dividend get cut in half?! No, not really. You're still getting 5 percent because you bought the stock at $20 rather than the current $40 price; the quoted yield is for investors who purchase Smith Co. today. They pay $40 and get the $1 dividend, and they're locked into the current yield of 2.5 percent. Although Smith Co. may have been a good income investment for you a month ago, it's not such a hot pick today because the price of the stock has doubled, cutting the yield in half. Even though the dividend hasn't changed, the yield has changed dramatically because of the stock price change.

>> **Stock price affects how good of an investment the stock may be.** Another way to look at yield is by looking at the investment amount. Using Smith Co. in Table 10-1 as the example, the investor who bought, say, 100 shares of Smith Co. when they were $20 per share paid only $2,000 (100 shares × $20 — leave out commissions to make the example simple). If the same stock is purchased later at $40 per share,

the total investment amount is $4,000 (100 shares × $40). In either case, the investor gets a total dividend income of $100 (100 shares × $1 dividend per share). Which investment is yielding more — the $2,000 investment or the $4,000 investment? Of course, it's better to get the income ($100 in this case) with the smaller investment (a 5 percent yield is better than a 2.5 percent yield).

Comparing yield between different stocks

All things being equal, choosing Smith Co. or Jones Co. is a coin toss. It's looking at your situation and each company's fundamentals and prospects that will sway you. What if Smith Co. is an auto stock (similar to General Motors in 2008) and Jones Co. is a utility serving the Las Vegas metro area? Now what? In 2008, the automotive industry struggled tremendously, but utilities were generally in much better shape. In that scenario, Smith Co.'s dividend is in jeopardy, whereas Jones Co.'s dividend is more secure. Another issue is the payout ratio (see the next section). Therefore, companies whose dividends have the same yield may still have different risks.

Looking at a stock's payout ratio

You can use the *payout ratio* to figure out what percentage of a company's earnings is being paid out in the form of dividends (Earnings = Sales − Expenses). Keep in mind that companies pay dividends from their net earnings. (Technically, the money comes from the company's capital accounts, but that money ultimately comes from net earnings and capital infusions.) Given that, the company's earnings should always be higher than the dividends the company pays out. An investor wants to see total earnings growth that exceeds the total amount paid for dividends. Here's how to figure a payout ratio:

Dividend (per share) ÷ Earnings (per share) = Payout ratio

Say that the company CashFlow Now, Inc., has annual earnings (or net income) of $1 million. Total dividends are to be paid out of $500,000, and the company has 1 million outstanding shares. Using those numbers, you know that CashFlow Now's earnings per share (EPS) are $1 ($1 million in earnings ÷ 1 million shares) and that it pays an annual dividend of 50 cents per share ($500,000 ÷ 1 million shares). The dividend payout ratio is

50 percent (the 50 cent dividend is 50 percent of the $1 EPS). This number is a healthy dividend payout ratio, because even if Cash-Flow Now's earnings fall by 10 percent or 20 percent, plenty of room still exists to pay dividends.

TIP

If you're concerned about your dividend income's safety, regularly watch the payout ratio. The maximum acceptable payout ratio should be 80 percent, and a good range is 50 to 70 percent. A payout ratio of 60 percent or lower is considered very safe (the lower the percentage, the safer the dividend).

REMEMBER

When a company suffers significant financial difficulties, its ability to pay dividends is compromised. Good examples of stocks that have had their dividends cut in recent years due to financial difficulties are mortgage companies in the wake of the housing bubble bursting and the fallout from the subprime debt fiasco. Mortgage companies received less and less income due to mortgage defaults, which forced the lowering of dividends as cash inflow shrank. So, if you need dividend income to help you pay your bills, you'd better be aware of the dividend payout ratio.

Studying a company's bond rating

Bond rating? Huh? What's that got to do with dividend-paying stocks? Actually, a company's bond rating is very important to income stock investors. The bond rating offers insight into the company's financial strength. Bonds get rated for quality for the same reasons that consumer agencies rate products like cars or toasters. S&P Global Ratings and Moody's are the major independent rating agencies that look into bond issuers. They look at the bond issuer and ask, "Does this bond issuer have the financial strength to pay back the bond and the interest as stipulated in the bond indenture?"

To understand why this rating is important, consider the following:

>> **A good bond rating means that the company is strong enough to pay its obligations.** These obligations include expenses, payments on debts, and declared dividends. If a bond rating agency gives the company a high rating (or if it raises the rating), that's a great sign for anyone holding the company's debt or receiving dividends.

>> **If a bond rating agency lowers the rating, that means the company's financial strength is deteriorating** — a red flag for anyone who owns the company's bonds or stock. A lower bond rating today may mean trouble for the dividend later on.

>> **A poor bond rating means that the company is having difficulty paying its obligations.** If the company can't pay all its obligations, it has to choose which ones to pay. More times than not, a financially troubled company chooses to cut dividends or (in a worst-case scenario) not pay dividends at all.

The highest rating issued by S&P is AAA. The grades AAA, AA, and A are considered *investment grade,* or of high quality. Bs and Cs indicate a medium grade, and anything lower than that is considered poor or very risky (the bonds are referred to as *junk bonds*). So, if you see an XXX rating, then, gee, you'd better stay away!

Diversifying your stocks

If most of your dividend income is from stock in a single company or single industry, consider reallocating your investment to avoid having all your eggs in one basket. Concerns about diversification apply to income stocks as well as growth stocks. If all your income stocks are in the electric utility industry, then any problems in that industry are potential problems for your portfolio as well. (Turn to Chapter 4 for more on risk.)

Exploring Some Typical Income Stocks

Although virtually every industry has stocks that pay dividends, some industries have more dividend-paying stocks than others. You won't find too many dividend-paying income stocks in the computer or biotech industries, for instance. The reason is that these types of companies need a lot of money to finance expensive research and development (R&D) projects to create new products. Without R&D, the company can't create new products to fuel sales, growth, and future earnings. Computer, biotech, and other innovative industries are better for growth investors. Keep reading for the scoop on stocks that work well for income investors.

It's electric! Utilities

Public utilities are among the stock market's most reliable dividend payers. They generate a large cash flow (if you don't believe me, look at your gas and electric bills!). Many investors have at least one utility company in their portfolio. Income-minded investors (especially retirees) should seriously consider utilities — and there are great utilities ETFs as well (see Chapter 11 for more on ETFs). Investing in your own local utility isn't a bad idea — at least it makes paying the utility bill less painful.

Before you invest in a public utility, consider the following:

REMEMBER

>> **The utility company's financial condition:** Is the company making money, and are its sales and earnings growing from year to year? Make sure the utility's bonds are rated A or higher (see the earlier section "Studying a company's bond rating").

>> **The company's dividend payout ratio:** Because utilities tend to have a good cash flow, don't be too concerned if the ratio reaches 70 percent. From a safety point of view, however, the lower the rate, the better. (See the earlier section "Looking at a stock's payout ratio" for more on payout ratios.)

>> **The company's geographic location:** If the utility covers an area that's doing well and offers an increasing population base and business expansion, that bodes well for your stock. A good resource for researching population and business data is the U.S. Census Bureau (www.census.gov).

An interesting mix: Real estate investment trusts

REITs are a special breed of stock. A *REIT* is an investment that has elements of both a stock and a *mutual fund* (a pool of money received from investors that's managed by an investment company):

>> A REIT resembles a stock in that it's a company whose stock is publicly traded on the major stock exchanges, and it has the usual features that you expect from a stock — it can be bought and sold easily through a broker, income is given to investors as dividends, and so on.

>> A REIT resembles a mutual fund in that it doesn't make its money selling goods and services; it makes its money by buying, selling, and managing an investment portfolio of real estate investments. It generates revenue from rents and property leases, as any landlord does. In addition, some REITs own mortgages, and they gain income from the interest.

REITs are called *trusts* only because they meet the requirements of the Real Estate Investment Trust Act of 1960. This act exempts REITs from corporate income tax and capital gains taxes as long as they meet certain criteria, such as dispensing 90 percent of their net income to shareholders. This provision is the reason why REITs generally issue generous dividends. Beyond this status, REITs are, in a practical sense, like any other publicly traded company.

The main advantages to investing in REITs include the following:

>> **Unlike other types of real estate investing, REITs are easy to buy and sell (REITs are more liquid than other types of traditional real estate investing).** You can buy a REIT by making a phone call to a broker or visiting a broker's website, just as you can to purchase any stock.

>> **REITs have higher-than-average yields.** Because they must distribute at least 90 percent of their income to shareholders, their dividends usually yield a return of 5 percent to 10 percent.

>> **REITs involve a lower risk than the direct purchase of real estate because they use a portfolio approach diversified among many properties.** Because you're investing in a company that buys the real estate, you don't have to worry about managing the properties — the company's management does that on a full-time basis. Usually, the REIT doesn't just manage one property; it's diversified in a portfolio of different properties.

>> **Investing in a REIT is affordable for small investors.** REIT shares usually trade in the $10 to $40 range, meaning that you can invest with very little money.

REITs do have disadvantages. Although they tend to be diversified with various properties, they're still susceptible to risks tied to the general real estate sector. Real estate investing reached manic, record-high levels during 2000–2007, which meant that a downturn was likely. Whenever you invest in an asset (like real estate or REITs in recent years) that has already skyrocketed due to artificial stimulants (in the case of real estate, very low interest rates and too much credit and debt), the potential losses can offset any potential (unrealized) income.

When you're looking for a REIT to invest in, analyze it the way you'd analyze a property. Look at the location and type of property. If shopping malls are booming in California and your REIT buys and sells shopping malls in California, then you'll probably do well. However, if your REIT invests in office buildings across the country and the office building market is overbuilt and having tough times, you'll have a tough time, too.

Many of the dangers of the "housing bubble" have passed, and investors can start looking at real estate investments (such as REITs) with less anxiety. However, choosing REITs with a view toward quality and strong fundamentals (location, potential rents, and so forth) is still a good idea.

Business development companies

For those seeking a relatively high dividend with some growth potential, consider taking a look at business development companies (BDCs). They sound a little arcane, but they can be bought as easily as a stock and their setup isn't that difficult to understand. A BDC is essentially a hybrid between a venture capital company and a mutual fund, and it trades like a closed-end fund. A *closed-end fund* functions like a regular mutual fund, but it's listed in the same way as a stock and has a finite number of total shares. Regular mutual funds are referred to as *open-ended,* which means that their shares are issued (or redeemed) and there is no finite number of shares as with closed-end funds.

Like a venture capital firm, a BDC invests in companies that are small or midsize and that need capital to grow in their early stages of development. A BDC is like a mutual fund in that it will invest in a batch of companies so there is some sense of diversification. The companies that the BDC invests in tend to be in a particular niche such as biotech, robotics, or another "sunrise" industry. As part of the financial structure, the companies receiving the funding from the BDC pay back the financing through higher fees and interest, so BDCs tend to have a high dividend.

Given that, a BDC can provide good dividend income, but keep in mind that there is higher risk because the companies are still in the early stages of development. For more details on BDCs, check out resources such as the following:

>> **CEF Connect:** www.cefconnect.com

>> **Closed-End Fund Advisors:** www.cefdata.com

>> **Closed-End Fund Association:** www.cefa.com

As of this writing, there are dozens of BDCs, so you can find more information on them in traditional stock-investing resources.

Covered Call Writing for Income

The world of options can be a little tricky (and can be very risky), but there is a relatively safe options strategy that any income-minded, conservative investor should consider (even if you're a retiree). Imagine a low-risk strategy that can easily boost your stock portfolio's cash flow by 5 percent, 7 percent, 9 percent, or even more. Yes, it's called *covered call writing*.

If you do covered call writing in a disciplined way, you won't lose money, but it does come with one risk: You may be forced to sell your asset (at a profit). What a risk!

Writing a covered call means that you, as the stock investor, enter into a buy/sell transaction (the *call*) whereby you (the seller or writer) will receive income (the *option premium*) in exchange for the potential obligation of selling your shares to the call buyer at a set price and time frame. If, say, you own 100 shares of a stock in your brokerage account at $45 per share, you could write a call option on these 100 shares where you may have an obligation to sell those shares at, say, $50 per share. In this example, the call buyer paid you a premium of, say, $100. If your shares don't reach the higher price of $50, you continue holding onto your shares, and you also keep the $100 you received. This call option is only for a relatively brief period of time (regular options typically expire in nine months or less, but there are long-dated options that have a shelf life beyond a year), so the price move would have to occur during the short life of the call option. If the call option expires before the stock reaches $50 (referred to as the *strike price*), then the call buyer has lost money, but the call writer gets to keep the cash received from the call option.

Covered call writing is a great way to generate extra income from your stocks. The only risk is that if the stock hits the strike price (in this case, $50 per share), the writer is obligated to sell the 100 shares at the elevated price of $50. Wow, such a risk — being obligated to sell your stock at a higher, more profitable share price!

TIP

For more comprehensive details on writing covered calls, see my book *High-Level Investing For Dummies* (Wiley).

Writing Puts for Income

Imagine earning income where the only risk is that you may be obligated to buy the stock of a company that you would like to own — at a lower price! I think that's cool. This sweet event can happen when you write a put option in your brokerage account.

When you write (sell) a put option, you receive income (the *premium*), and in exchange you have an obligation — you're required to purchase the underlying security at the option's strike price. Say that there is a $50 stock you like, but you would like to purchase it at a lower price, such as $45. In that case, you write a put option with the strike price of $45. You receive the premium income (say, $200 in this example). If the stock doesn't go down to $45 during the option time frame, the option would expire, and the good news is that you keep the $200 as income (cool!). If the stock goes down to $45 (or lower) during the time frame of the put option, you're required to buy the stock at $45. The good news is that you end up buying a stock you like at a discount (cool again!). Why? Because you really end up paying $4,300 for the underlying stock. The breakdown is that the stock costs $4,500 (100 shares × $45), but you also received $200 in put option income, meaning that your total outlay of funds was only $4,300 ($4,500 – $200).

TIP

Given that, we come to the first golden rule of writing put options: Only write a put option on a stock (or ETF) that you would *love* to own anyway. Think of stocks that you consider an excellent addition to your brokerage portfolio. Say that the stock you're strongly considering is at $40 per share, and you'd be happy to own it at $35 per share.

TIP

For more in-depth information on writing put options, check out my book *High-Level Investing For Dummies* (Wiley).

Chapter **11**

Exploring Exchange-Traded Funds

W hen it comes to stock investing, there's more than one way to do it. Buying stocks directly is good; sometimes, buying stocks indirectly is equally good (or even better) — especially if you're risk averse. Buying a great stock is every stock investor's dream, but sometimes you face investing environments that make finding a winning stock a hazardous pursuit. In this day and age, prudent stock investors should definitely consider adding *exchange-traded funds* (ETFs) to their wealth-building arsenal.

An ETF is basically a mutual fund that invests in a fixed basket of securities but with a few twists. In this chapter, I show you how ETFs are similar to (and different from) mutual funds, provide some pointers on picking ETFs, and note the fundamentals of stock indexes (which are connected to ETFs).

Comparing Exchange-Traded Funds and Mutual Funds

For many folks and for many years, the only choice besides investing directly in stocks was to invest indirectly through mutual funds. After all, why buy a single stock for roughly the same few thousand dollars that you can buy a mutual fund for and get benefits such as professional management and diversification?

For small investors, mutual-fund investing isn't a bad way to go. Investors participate by pooling their money with others and get professional money management in an affordable manner. But mutual funds have their downsides, too. Mutual-fund fees, which include management fees and sales charges (referred to as *loads*), eat into gains, and investors have no choice about investments after they're in a mutual fund. Whatever the fund manager buys, sells, or holds onto is pretty much what the investors in the fund have to tolerate. Investment choice is limited to either being in the fund or out.

But now, with the advent of ETFs, investors have greater choices than ever, a scenario that sets the stage for the inevitable comparison between mutual funds and ETFs. The following sections go over the differences and similarities between ETFs and mutual funds.

The differences

Simply stated, in a mutual fund, securities such as stocks and bonds are constantly bought, sold, and held (in other words, the fund is *actively managed*). An ETF holds similar securities, but the portfolio typically isn't actively managed. Instead, an ETF usually holds a fixed basket of securities that may reflect an index or a particular industry or sector (see Chapter 12). An *index* is a method of measuring the value of a segment of the general stock market. It's a tool used by money managers and investors to compare the performance of a particular stock to a widely accepted standard (see the later section "Taking Note of Indexes" for more details).

For example, an ETF that tries to reflect the S&P 500 will attempt to hold a securities portfolio that mirrors the composition of the S&P 500 as closely as possible. Here's another example: A water utilities ETF may hold the top 35 or 40 publicly held water companies. (You get the picture.)

REMEMBER

Where ETFs are markedly different from mutual funds (and where they're really advantageous, in my opinion) is that they can be bought and sold like stocks. In addition, you can do with ETFs what you can generally do with stocks (but can't usually do with mutual funds): You can buy in share allotments, such as 1, 50, or 100 shares or more. Mutual funds, on the other hand, are usually bought in dollar amounts, such as $1,000 or $5,000. The dollar amount you can initially invest is set by the manager of the individual mutual fund.

Here are some other advantages: You can put various buy/sell brokerage orders on ETFs (see Chapter 13), and many ETFs are *optionable* (meaning you may be able to buy or sell put and call options on them; I discuss some strategies with options in Chapter 16). Mutual funds typically aren't optionable. I cover put and call options extensively in my book *High-Level Investing For Dummies* (Wiley).

WARNING

Keep in mind that put and call options are typically very speculative, so use them sparingly, and find out as much as possible about their pros and cons before you decide to use them in your stock-investing account. Keep in mind that most option strategies are usually not allowed in stock/ETF portfolios within retirement accounts.

In addition, many ETFs are *marginable* (meaning that you can borrow against them with some limitations in your brokerage account). Mutual funds usually aren't marginable when purchased directly (although it is possible if they're within the confines of a stock brokerage account). To find out more about margins, check out Chapter 13.

REMEMBER

Sometimes an investor can readily see the great potential of a given industry or sector but is hard-pressed to get that single really good stock that can take advantage of the profit possibilities of that particular segment of the market. The great thing about an ETF is that you can make that investment very easily, knowing that if you're unsure about it, you can put in place strategies that protect you from the downside (such as stop-loss orders or trailing stops). That way, you can sleep more easily!

The similarities

Even though ETFs and mutual funds have some major differences, they do share a few similarities:

>> ETFs and mutual funds are similar in that they aren't direct investments; they're "conduits" of investing, which means that they act like a connection between the investor and the investments.

>> Both ETFs and mutual funds basically pool the money of investors and the pool becomes the "fund," which, in turn, invests in a portfolio of investments.

>> Both ETFs and mutual funds offer the great advantage of diversification (although they accomplish it in different ways).

>> Investors don't have any choice about what makes up the portfolio of either the ETF or the mutual fund. The ETF has a fixed basket of securities (the money manager overseeing the portfolio makes those choices), and, of course, investors can't control the choices made in a mutual fund.

TIP

For those investors who want more active assistance in making choices and running a portfolio, the mutual fund may very well be the way to go. For those who are more comfortable making their own choices in terms of the particular index or industry/sector they want to invest in, the ETF may be a better venue.

Choosing an Exchange-Traded Fund

Buying a stock is an investment in a particular company, but an ETF is an opportunity to invest in a block of stocks. In the same way a few mouse clicks can buy you a stock at a stock brokerage website, those same clicks can buy you virtually an entire industry or sector (or at least the top-tier stocks in an industry or sector).

For investors who are comfortable with their own choices and do their due diligence, a winning stock is a better (albeit more aggressive) way to go. For those investors who want to make their own choices but aren't that confident about picking winning stocks, an ETF is definitely a better way to go.

You had to figure that choosing an ETF wasn't going to be a coin flip. There are considerations that you should be aware of, some of which are tied more to your personal outlook and preferences than to the underlying portfolio of the ETF. I give you the info you need on bullish and bearish ETFs in the following sections.

TIP

Picking a winning industry or sector is easier than finding a great company to invest in. Therefore, ETF investing goes hand in hand with the guidance I offer in Chapter 12.

Bullish ETFs

You may wake up one day and say, "I think that the stock market will do very well going forward from today," and that's just fine if you think so. Maybe your research on the general economy, financial outlook, and political considerations makes you feel happier than a starving man on a cruise ship. But you just don't know (or don't care to research) which stocks would best benefit from the good market moves yet to come. No problem!

In the following sections, I cover ETF strategies for bullish scenarios, but fortunately, ETF strategies for bearish scenarios exist, too. I cover those later in this chapter.

Major market index ETFs

Why not invest in ETFs that mirror a general major market index such as the S&P 500? ETFs such as SPY construct their portfolios to track the composition of the S&P 500 as closely as possible. As they say, why try to beat the market when you can match it? It's a great way to go when the market is having a good rally. (See the later section "Taking Note of Indexes" for the basics on indexes.)

When the S&P 500 was battered in late 2008 and early 2009, the ETF for the S&P 500, of course, mirrored that performance and hit the bottom in March 2009. But from that moment on and into 2015, the S&P 500 (and the ETFs that tracked it) did extraordinarily well. It paid to buck the bearish sentiment of early 2009. Of course, it did take some contrarian gumption to do so, but at least you had the benefit of the full S&P 500 stock portfolio, which at least had more diversification than a single stock or a single subsection of the market. Of course, as the S&P 500 entered the bull market of 2009–2015, bullish ETFs that mirrored the S&P 500 did very well, while the ETFs that were *inverse* to the S&P 500 (betting on a bearish move) declined in the same period.

ETFs related to human need

Some ETFs cover industries such as food and beverage, water, energy, and other things that people will keep buying no matter how good or bad the economy is. Without needing a crystal ball or having an iron-will contrarian attitude, a stock investor can simply put money into stocks — or in this case, ETFs — tied to human need. Such ETFs may even do better than ETFs tied to major market indexes (see the preceding section).

Here's an example: At the end of 2007 (mere months before the great 2008–2009 market crash), what would've happened if you had invested 50 percent of your money in an ETF that represented the S&P 500 and 50 percent in an ETF that was in consumer staples (such as food and beverage stocks)? I did such a comparison, and it was quite revealing to note that by the end of 2015, the consumer staples ETF (for the record, I used one with the securities symbol PBJ) actually beat out the S&P 500 ETF by more than 45 percent (not including dividends). Very interesting!

ETFs that include dividend-paying stocks

ETFs don't necessarily have to be tied to a specific industry or sector; they can be tied to a specific type or subcategory of stock. All things being equal, what basic categories of stocks do you think would better weather bad times: stocks with no dividends or stocks that pay dividends? (I guess the question answers itself, pretty much like, "What tastes better: apple pie or barbed wire?") Although some sectors are known for being good dividend payers, such as utilities (and there are some good ETFs that cover this industry), some ETFs cover stocks that meet specific criteria.

You can find ETFs that include high-dividend income stocks (typically 3.5 percent or higher), as well as ETFs that include stocks of companies that don't necessarily pay high dividends but do have a long track record of dividend increases that meet or exceed the rate of inflation.

TIP

Given these types of dividend-paying ETFs, it becomes clear which is good for what type of stock investor:

>> **If I were a stock investor who was currently retired, I'd choose the high-dividend stock ETF.** Dividend-paying stock ETFs are generally more stable than stock ETFs that don't pay dividends, and dividends are important for retirement income.

>> **If I were in *pre-retirement* (some years away from retirement but clearly planning for it), I'd choose the ETF with the stocks that had a strong record of growing the dividend payout.** That way, those same dividend-paying stocks would grow in the short term and provide better income down the road during retirement.

For more information on dividend investing strategies (and other income ideas), head to Chapter 10.

REMEMBER Keep in mind that dividend–paying stocks generally fall within the criteria of human need investing because those companies tend to be large and stable, with good cash flows, giving them the ongoing wherewithal to pay good dividends.

TIP To find out more about ETFs in general and to get more details on the ETFs I mention in this chapter, go to websites such as `https://etfdb.com` and `www.etfguide.com`.

Bearish ETFs

Most ETFs are bullish in nature because they invest in a portfolio of securities that they expect to go up in due course. But some ETFs have a bearish focus. Bearish ETFs (also called *short ETFs*) maintain a portfolio of securities and strategies that are designed to go the opposite way of the underlying or targeted securities. In other words, this type of ETF goes up when the underlying securities go down (and vice versa). Bearish ETFs employ securities such as *put options* (and similar derivatives) and/or employ strategies such as going short (see Chapter 13).

Take the S&P 500, for example. If you were bullish on that index, you might choose an ETF such as SPY. However, if you were bearish on that index and wanted to seek gains by betting that it would go down, you could choose an ETF such as SH.

You can take two approaches on bearish ETFs:

>> **Hoping for a downfall:** If you're speculating on a pending market crash, a bearish ETF is a good consideration. In this approach, you're actually seeking to make a profit based on your expectations. Those folks who aggressively went into bearish ETFs during early or mid-2008 made some spectacular profits during the tumultuous downfall during late 2008 and early 2009.

> **» Hedging against a downfall:** A more conservative approach is to use bearish ETFs to a more moderate extent, primarily as a form of hedging, whereby the bearish ETF acts like a form of insurance in the unwelcome event of a significant market pullback or crash. I say "unwelcome" because you're not really hoping for a crash; you're just trying to protect yourself with a modest form of diversification. In this context, diversification means that you have a mix of both bullish positions and, to a smaller extent, bearish positions.

Taking Note of Indexes

For stock investors, ETFs that are bullish or bearish are ultimately tied to major market indexes. You should take a quick look at indexes to better understand them (and the ETFs tied to them).

Whenever you hear the media commentary or the scuttlebutt at the local watering hole about "how the market is doing," it typically refers to a market proxy such as an index. You'll usually hear them mention "the Dow" or perhaps "the S&P 500." There are certainly other major market indexes, and there are many lesser, yet popular, measurements, such as the Dow Jones Transportation Average. Indexes and averages tend to be used interchangeably, but they're distinctly different entities of measurement.

Most people use these indexes basically as standards of market performance to see whether they're doing better or worse than a yardstick for comparison purposes. They want to know continuously whether their stocks, ETFs, mutual funds, or overall portfolios are performing well.

TIP

You can find great resources online at sites such as www.dowjones.com, www.spglobal.com/spdji, and www.investopedia.com, which give you the history and composition of indexes. For your purposes, these are the main ones to keep an eye on:

> **» Dow Jones Industrial Average (DJIA):** This is the most widely watched index (technically, it's not an index, but it's utilized as one). It tracks 30 widely owned, large-cap stocks, and it's occasionally rebalanced to drop (and replace) a stock that's not keeping up.

>> **Nasdaq Composite:** This covers a cross section of stocks from the Nasdaq. It's generally considered a mix of stocks that are high-growth (riskier) companies with an overrepresentation of technology stocks.

>> **S&P 500 Index:** This index tracks 500 leading, publicly traded companies considered to be widely held. The publishing firm Standard & Poor's created this index (I bet you could've guessed that).

>> **Wilshire 5000:** This index is considered the widest sampling of stocks across the general stock market and, therefore, a more accurate measure of stock-market movement.

TIP

If you don't want to go nuts trying to "beat the market," consider an ETF that closely correlates to any of the indexes mentioned in the preceding list. Sometimes it's better to join 'em than to beat 'em. You can find ETFs that track or mirror the preceding indexes at sites such as https://etfdb.com.

INTERNATIONAL INVESTING MADE EASY

Interested in investing in stocks on the international scene? Does Europe, China, or India interest you? Perhaps Singapore or Australia appeals to you, but finding a good stock seems a little daunting. Why not do it in a safer way through ETFs? Many ETFs invest in a cross section of the major stocks in a given country. So, why buy an individual stock when you can get the top 40 or 50 stocks in that country's stock market?

In this chapter, you discover the advantages of ETFs, so including a batch of international stocks in your portfolio is easier than ever. To find major international ETFs, go to https://etfdb.com, and use the country's name in your keyword search. Just remember to do your homework on that country (geopolitical risks and so on) with the help of the *Financial Times* (www.ft.com). Of course, if you get skittish about holding such ETFs, you can minimize the risks with techniques such as stop-loss orders (see Chapter 13).

Chapter **12**

Surveying Emerging Sector and Industry Opportunities

Suppose you have to bet your entire nest egg on a one-mile race. All you need to do is select a winning group. Your choices are the following:

Group A: Thoroughbred racehorses

Group B: Overweight Elvis impersonators

Group C: Lethargic snails

This isn't a trick question, and you have one minute to answer. Notice that I didn't ask you to pick a single winner out of a giant mush of horses, Elvii, and snails; I only asked you to pick the winning group in the race. The obvious answer is the thoroughbred racehorses (and no, they weren't ridden by the overweight Elvis impersonators because that would take away from the eloquent point I'm making). In this example, even the slowest member of Group A easily outdistances the fastest member of either Group B or Group C.

Industries (like Groups A, B, and C in my example) aren't equal, and life isn't fair. After all, if life were fair, Elvis would be alive, and the impersonators wouldn't exist. Fortunately, picking stocks doesn't have to be as difficult as picking a winning racehorse. The basic point is that it's easier to pick a successful stock from a group of winners (a growing, vibrant industry). Understanding industries only enhances your stock-picking strategy.

A successful, long-term investor looks at the industry (or the basic sector) just as carefully as they look at the individual stock. Luckily, choosing a winning industry to invest in is easier than choosing individual stocks, as you find out in this chapter. I know some investors who can pick a winning stock in a losing industry, and I also know investors who've chosen a losing stock in a winning industry (the former is far outnumbered by the latter). Just think how well you do when you choose a great stock in a great industry! Of course, if you repeatedly choose bad stocks in bad industries, you may as well get out of the stock market altogether (maybe your calling is to be a celebrity impersonator instead!).

Telling the Difference between a Sector and an Industry

Very often, investors confuse an industry with a sector. Even though it may not be a consequential confusion, some clarity is needed here.

REMEMBER

A *sector* is simply a group of interrelated industries. An *industry* is typically a category of business that performs a more precise activity; you can call an industry a *subsector.* Investing in a sector and investing in an industry can mean different things for the investor. The result of your investment performance can also be very different.

Health care is a good example of a sector that has different industries. The sector of health care includes such industries as pharmaceuticals, drug retailers, health insurance, hospitals, medical equipment manufacturers, and so on.

REMEMBER

Health care is actually a good example of why you should know the distinction between a sector and an industry. Within a given sector (like health care), you have industries that behave differently during the same economic conditions. Some of the industries are cyclical (like medical equipment manufacturers), whereas some are defensive (like drug retailers). In a bad economy, cyclicals tend to go down, while defensive stocks tend to hold their value. In a good or booming economy, cyclicals do very well, while defensive stocks tend to lag behind. (I talk more about cyclical and defensive industries later in this chapter.)

Given that fact, an exchange-traded fund (ETF) that reflected the general health-care sector would be generally flat because some of the industries that went up would be offset by those that went down. (Turn to Chapter 11 for more about ETFs.)

Interrogating the Sectors and Industries

Your common sense is an important tool in choosing sectors and industries with winning stocks. This section explores some of the most important questions to ask yourself when you're choosing a sector or industry.

Which category does the industry fall into?

Most industries can neatly be placed in one of two categories: cyclical or defensive. In a rough way, these categories generally translate into what society wants and what it needs. Society buys what it *wants* when times are good and holds off when times are bad. It buys what it *needs* in both good and bad times. A want is a "like to have," whereas a need is a "must have." Got it?

Cyclical industries

Cyclical industries are industries whose fortunes rise and fall with the economy's rise and fall. In other words, if the economy and the stock market are doing well, consumers and investors are confident and tend to spend and invest more money than usual, so cyclical industries tend to do well. Real estate and automobiles are great examples of cyclical industries.

Your own situation offers you some common-sense insight into the concept of cyclical industries. Think about your behavior as a consumer, and you get a revealing clue into the thinking of millions of consumers. When you (and millions of others) feel good about your career, your finances, and your future, you have a greater tendency to buy more (and/or more expensive) stuff. When people feel financially strong, they're more apt to buy a new house or car or make some other large financial commitment. Also, people take on more debt because they feel confident that they can pay it back. In light of this behavior, what industries do you think would do well?

The same point holds for business spending. When businesses think that economic times are good and foresee continuing good times, they tend to spend more money on large purchases such as new equipment or technology. They think that when they're doing well and are flush with financial success, it's a good idea to reinvest that money in the business to increase future success.

Defensive industries

Defensive industries are industries that produce goods and services that are needed no matter what's happening in the economy. Your common sense kicks in here, too. What do you buy even when times are tough? Think about what millions of people buy no matter how bad the economy gets. A good example is food — people still need to eat regardless of good or bad times. Other examples of defensive industries are utilities and health care.

REMEMBER

In bad economic times, defensive stocks tend to do better than cyclical stocks. However, when times are good, cyclical stocks tend to do better than defensive stocks. Defensive stocks don't do as well in good times because people don't necessarily eat twice as much or use up more electricity.

So, how do defensive stocks grow? Their growth generally relies on two factors:

>> **Population growth:** As more and more consumers are born, more people become available to buy.

>> **New markets:** A company can grow by seeking out new groups of consumers to buy its products and services. Coca-Cola, for example, found new markets in Asia during

the 1990s. As communist regimes fell from power and more societies embraced a free market and consumer goods, the company sold more beverages and its stock soared.

TIP

One way to invest in a particular industry is to take advantage of ETFs, which have become very popular in recent years. ETFs are structured much like mutual funds but are fixed portfolios that trade like a stock. If you find a winning industry, but you can't find a winning stock (or don't want to bother with the necessary research), then ETFs are a great consideration. You can find out more about ETFs on websites such as https://etfdb.com or by turning to Chapter 11.

Is the sector growing?

This question may seem obvious, but you still need to ask it before you purchase stock. The saying "the trend is your friend" applies when choosing a sector in which to invest, as long as the trend is an upward one. If you look at three different stocks that are equal in every significant way, but you find that one stock is in a sector growing 15 percent per year while the other two stocks are in sectors that either have little growth or are shrinking, which stock would you choose?

WARNING

Sometimes the stock of a financially unsound or poorly run company goes up dramatically because the sector it's in is very exciting to the public. A recent example is marijuana stocks during 2018–2019. Their stock prices generally soared during 2018, but generally crashed during 2019. Investors and speculators went nuts buying up stocks as widespread legalization by key states opened the floodgates of interest. However, stock prices came down significantly from their highs (you were expecting a pun, right?), and investors soon smelled the coffee and remembered that fundamentals matter (as they eventually do!). Whatever new area interests you, be sure to look at the company's fundamentals (see Chapter 6 to find out how to do this) and the prospects for the industry's growth before settling on a particular stock.

TIP

To judge how well a sector or industry is doing, various information sources monitor all the sectors and industries and measure their progress. Some reliable sources include the following:

>> **D&B Hoovers:** www.hoovers.com

>> **MarketWatch:** www.marketwatch.com

>> **S&P Global Ratings:** www.spglobal.com/ratings

>> *The Wall Street Journal:* www.wsj.com

>> **Yahoo! Finance:** https://finance.yahoo.com

The preceding sources generally give you in-depth information about the major sectors and industries. Visit their websites to read their current research and articles and get links to relevant sites for more details. For example, *The Wall Street Journal* (published by Dow Jones & Co.), whose website is updated daily (or more frequently), publishes indexes for all the major sectors and industries so you can get a useful snapshot of how well each one is doing.

TIP

Standard and Poor's (S&P) Industry Survey are an excellent source of information on U.S. industries. Besides ranking and comparing industries and informing you about their current prospects, the survey also lists the top companies by size, sales, earnings, and other key information. What I like is that each industry is covered in a few pages, so you get the critical information you need without reading a novel. The survey and other S&P publications are available on the S&P website or in the business reference section of most libraries (the library is your best bet because the survey is rather expensive).

Will demand for the sector's products and/or services see long-term growth?

Look at the products and services that the sector or industry provides. Do they look like things that society will continue to want? Are there products and services on the horizon that could replace them? What does the foreseeable future look like for the sector?

REMEMBER

When evaluating future demand, look for a *sunrise industry* — one that's new or emerging or has promising appeal for the future. Good examples of sunrise industries in recent years are biotech and internet companies. In contrast, a *sunset industry* is one that either is declining or has little potential for growth. For example, you probably shouldn't invest in the DVD manufacturing industry because demand has shifted toward digital delivery instead. Owning stock in a strong, profitable company in a sunrise industry is obviously the most desirable choice.

Current research unveils the following megatrends:

>> **The aging of the United States:** More senior citizens than ever before are living in the United States. Because of this fact, health care and financial services that touch on eldercare or financial concerns of the elderly will prosper.

>> **Advances in high technology:** Artificial intelligence (AI), telecom, medical, and biotechnology innovations will continue.

>> **Security concerns:** Terrorism, international tensions, and security issues on a personal level mean more attention for national defense, homeland security, and related matters.

>> **Energy challenges:** Traditional and nontraditional sources of energy (such as solar, fuel cells, and so on) will demand society's attention as it transitions from fossil fuels to new forms of energy.

TIP

One of my favorite resources for anticipating megatrends is Gerald Celente and his *Trends Journal* (https://trendsjournal.com). They've been spot-on with forecasting megatrends as they unfold.

What does the industry's growth rely on?

An industry doesn't exist in a vacuum. External factors weigh heavily on an industry's ability to survive and thrive. Does the industry rely on an established megatrend? Then it will probably be strong for a while. Does it rely on factors that are losing relevance? Then it may begin to decline soon. Technological and demographic changes are other factors that may contribute to an industry's growth or fall.

REMEMBER

Keep in mind that a sector will continue to grow, shrink, or be level, but individual industries can grow, shrink, or even be on a track to disappear. If a sector is expanding, you may see new industries emerge. For example, the graying of the United States is an established megatrend. As millions of Americans climb into their later years, profitable opportunities await companies that are prepared to cater to them. Perhaps an industry (subsector) offers great new medical products for senior citizens. What are the prospects for growth?

Does the industry depend on another industry?

This twist on the prior question is a reminder that industries frequently are intertwined and can become codependent. When one industry suffers, you may find it helpful to understand which industries will subsequently suffer. The reverse can also be true: When one industry is doing well, other industries may reap the benefits.

In either case, if the stock you choose is in an industry that's highly dependent on other industries, you should know about it. If you're considering stocks of resort companies and you see the headlines blaring, "Airlines losing money as public stops flying," what do you do? This type of question forces you to think logically and consider cause and effect. Logic and common sense are powerful tools that frequently trump all the number-crunching activities performed by analysts.

Who are the leading companies in the industry?

After you've chosen the industry, what types of companies do you want to invest in? You can choose from two basic types:

>> **Established leaders:** These companies are considered industry leaders or have a large share of the market. Investing in these companies is the safer way to go; what better choice for novice investors than companies that have already proven themselves?

>> **Innovators:** If the industry is hot and you want to be more aggressive in your approach, investigate companies that offer new products, patents, or technologies. These companies are probably smaller but have a greater potential for growth in a proven industry.

Is the industry a target of government action?

You need to know whether the government is targeting an industry because intervention by politicians and bureaucrats (rightly or wrongly) can have an impact on an industry's economic situation.

Find out about any political issues that face a company, industry, or sector.

WARNING

Investors need to take heed when political "noise" starts coming out about a particular industry. An industry can be hurt either by direct government intervention or by the threat of it. Intervention can take the form of lawsuits, investigations, taxes, regulations, or sometimes an outright ban. In any case, being on the wrong end of government intervention is the greatest external threat to a company's survival.

REMEMBER

Sometimes, government action helps an industry. Generally, beneficial action takes two forms:

>> **Deregulation and/or tax decreases:** Government sometimes reduces burdens on an industry. During the late 1990s, for example, government deregulation led the way to more innovation in the telecommunications industry. This trend, in turn, laid the groundwork for more innovation and growth in the internet and expansion of cellphone service.

>> **Direct funding:** Government has the power to steer taxpayer money toward business as well. In recent years, federal and state governments have provided tax credits and other incentives for alternative energy such as solar power.

Outlining Key Sectors and Industries

In this section, I highlight some up-and-coming sectors and industries that investors should take note of, as well as established sectors and industries that have strong potential for the coming years. Consider investing some of your stock portfolio in those that look promising (and, of course, avoid those that look problematic).

REMEMBER

Keep in mind everything you read in earlier chapters (like Chapters 6 and 7) regarding the fundamentals (sales, profits, and so on) of the best companies within these sectors and industries. No matter how new, glamourous, and popular some companies seem to be, always go back to the fundamentals. Don't get excited when you hear pundits say that these companies or trends are "groundbreaking" with "game-changing" technologies or "glitzy" inventions.

The internet in the late 1990s, for example, was, indeed, extremely significant for the economy and society at large, but the initial wave of companies ultimately had more losers than winners. Hundreds of dot-com companies ended up in the graveyard of barely remembered failures. The real growth opportunities emerged with the second wave, which meant those companies that survived made a profit and went on to become leaders of the pack.

Robotics and artificial intelligence

Robotics and AI are promising new areas of growth in the economy. Companies big and small are getting in on the action. This technology ranges from drones to actual, lifelike robots. The growth in this technology has been tremendous, and because there are so many applications for it, ranging from robots that perform basic services to military uses such as defusing bombs and other traditionally hazardous tasks, growth in this venue looks strong going forward.

TIP

My favorite way to invest in this venue is through ETFs so that I can invest in a wide swath of companies; the industry has strong growth prospects, but it's not always easy to discern winning individual companies. For individual companies to choose from, why not take a look at the top holdings of a robotics ETF? A good example of a leading robotics ETF is ROBO (the ROBO Global Robotics and Automation Index ETF). When you see some suitable companies in an ETF, review their fundamentals before you add them to your growth portfolio. Turn to Chapter 11 for more about ETFs; Chapters 6 and 7 are a good start for reviewing company fundamentals.

Ecommerce

Amazon is considered the quintessential e-commerce site as more and more of the public are turning to the internet for their consumer purchases. I think that Amazon stock is very expensive — not only on a per-share basis but also based on fundamentals. (It has a very high P/E ratio; compare it to others by reading up on P/E ratios in Chapter 5.) I think there are better ways to profit from ecommerce.

TIP

Consider companies that make money every time someone buys something online such as Visa or PayPal. And yes, there are ETFs in this venue, too.

Commodities

In the year 2000, the general commodities complex entered a multiyear bull market and resulted in some spectacular gains for early investors. Then the mega crisis of 2008 hit, and commodities collapsed. As economies struggled and contracted, demand for general commodities was generally down, and stocks and ETFs tied to this sector sputtered and declined in the ensuing years. But a commodities bull market for 2022–2025 looks good and worth investigating.

Keep in mind that commodities do not move in lockstep — some commodities can do well when others do not. Supply-and-demand factors are primary considerations. Commodities tied to food (such as grains), for example, tend to keep growing moderately as investment vehicles as the world population continues to grow. Commodities tied to building and infrastructure (such as base metals like copper and zinc), on the other hand, tend to do well when good economic times translate into more things being built such as highways, skyscrapers, and so forth. Energy-related commodities (such as oil and natural gas) do well when the economy is booming and demand for energy increases.

How to play commodities? Of course, many people assume that commodities are all about trading and speculating, but there are plenty of ways for stock investors to participate. Virtually every major commodity has a variety of ways for you to play it.

If you believe that soybeans will be doing very well in the coming years, you can invest in a company such as Bunge Ltd., or you can do the ETF in soybeans (the Teucrium Soybean fund). If you think that corn will do well and you want to stalk some profits there (see what I did?), you can consider companies such as Archer Daniels Midland or the corn ETF (the Teucrium Corn Fund). If you think grains in general will do well but you're not sure which ones will have more fertile profits, consider ETFs exposed to grains such as DBA (the Invesco DB Agriculture Fund). It has soybeans and corn but also includes wheat and even cattle and hogs, too.

Precious metals

The time we're experiencing (circa 2023–2024) is unique and dangerous in its scope and risk. Trillions in debt, the greatest in our history. This massive debt load includes both the public and private sectors and is international. The overproduction of global currencies such as the U.S. dollar, the euro, and China's yuan is greater than ever. The world's banking systems are very shaky. The condition of counterparty risk in every major paper asset class is at an all-time high. What's an investor to do?

In my book *Investing in Gold & Silver For Dummies* (Wiley), I detail the problems with paper assets and the need to diversify with assets that don't have counter-party risk, such as gold and silver. These precious metals are an important hedge in the case of financial crises tied to paper assets. Paper assets, such as bonds (government, corporate, and so on), are reaching unsustainable levels, which could have dangerous effects on many portfolios and retirement accounts. Additionally, central banks such as the Federal Reserve typically resort to opening up the spigots for cash and more debt in attempts to placate any looming financial crisis.

Given that, hard-asset alternatives tend to be treated by the investing public as safe harbors. Precious metals did very well in the late 1970s when inflation and an energy crisis erupted, they repeated their bullish runs during 2000–2010, and they're doing well for 2023–2030.

For stock and ETF investors, there are plenty of good choices to add exposure to the world of gold and silver. Good examples of precious metals ETFs are SPDR Gold Shares and iShares Silver Trust. To find out more about precious metals (along with stocks and ETFs related to them), take a look at *Investing in Gold & Silver For Dummies.*

Cryptocurrency opportunities

Cryptocurrencies have recently established themselves as an aggressive alternative to currencies in recent years, but they've proven to be risky and volatile. It was an incredible bubble that pushed cryptocurrencies such as Bitcoin soaring to a unit value of $13,800 during late 2017 and early 2018 and then crashing to $3,500 by the start of 2019. Then it soared again to $10,000 before falling to $7,300 at the end of 2019. They crashed again in 2022 and have recovered in early 2023. I'm getting dizzy just writing about this roller-coaster ride, but for those speculators who are interested (this area is not about investing!), do your homework.

TIP

Investing (actually, speculating) in cryptocurrencies is not for the fainthearted and should be done only with a relatively small portion of your investable funds. Given that, here are two considerations for you:

>> If you want to be involved with cryptocurrencies, find out about using them as a transactional medium and not an investment vehicle. This means that if you have a business — even a part-time one from home or through freelancing — consider making it a payment option so you can receive, say, Bitcoin as a payment for your services.

>> If you want to invest, consider companies that make money from the products and services tied to cryptocurrencies such as blockchain technology. That way you can participate in the growth of cryptocurrencies with less exposure to their risks and volatility.

TIP

My favorite resource for folks who are beginners and are serious about getting directly involved with cryptocurrencies is the book *Cryptocurrency Investing For Dummies* by Kiana Danial (Wiley).

Driving it home

We need to get investors to slow down after reading all those headlines about how electric vehicles (EVs) will soon be taking over the driving world. Watch out for the Yield sign up ahead! Yes, companies such as Tesla have become the darlings of the auto world, but investors are better off pumping the brakes.

A growing consensus among automotive analysts and researchers is that these vehicles do have problems and that they aren't as good for the environment as proponents first argued. Although this chapter lists some great megatrends for investors to take note of, in this section, I consider EVs to be a cautionary tale. These vehicles are problematic, unreliable, and very expensive. They take too much time to recharge and the upkeep (repairs and so on) is very expensive. From late 2022 to early 2023, automotive consumers slowly but surely became resistant to them and sales went down. So, what is an investor to do?

First, don't consider EV stocks to be a good or reliable investment (yet). The sales and earnings must materialize before you should consider investing. Stock investors are better off waiting for the next round of improvements before they take a test-drive with their investment portfolio dollars.

A second take on this topic is to do the "picks and pans" approach. If the automotive industry will be investing billions in EVs, a safer way to profit will be to learn which commodities (such as lithium and graphite) will benefit from this and do your research on those opportunities.

Chapter **13**

Looking at Brokerage Orders and Trading Techniques

Investment success isn't just about which stocks to choose; it's also about how you choose those stocks. Frequently, investors think that good stock picking means doing your homework and then making that buy (or sell). However, you can take it a step further to maximize profits (or minimize losses).

In 2008, millions of investors were slammed mercilessly by a tumultuous market; many could've used some simple techniques and orders that could've saved them some grief. Investors who used stop-loss orders avoided some of the trillion-dollar carnage that hit the stock market during that scary time. As a stock investor, you can take advantage of this technique and others available through your standard brokerage account (see Chapter 8). This chapter presents some of the best ways you can use these powerful techniques, which are useful whether you're buying or selling stock.

Checking Out Brokerage Orders

Orders you place with your stockbroker fit neatly into three categories:

» Time-related orders

» Condition-related orders

» Advanced orders (which are combinations of the preceding two)

At the very least, get familiar with the first two types of orders because they're easy to implement, and they're invaluable tools for wealth building and (more important) wealth saving!

TIP

Using a combination of orders helps you fine-tune your strategy so you can maintain greater control over your investments. Speak with your broker about the different types of orders you can use to maximize the gains (or minimize the losses) from your stock-investing activities. You also can read the broker's policies on stock orders at the brokerage website.

Time-related orders

A *time-related order* is just that — the order has a time limit. Typically, investors use these orders in conjunction with condition-related orders, which I describe later in this chapter. The two most common time-related orders are day orders and good-'til-canceled (GTC) orders.

Day orders

A *day order* is an order to buy or sell a stock that expires at the end of that particular trading day. If you tell your broker, "Buy BYOB, Inc., at $37.50, and make it a day order," you mean that you want to purchase the stock at $37.50. But if the stock doesn't hit that price, your order expires, unfilled, at the end of the trading day.

Why would you place such an order? Maybe BYOB is trading at $39, but you don't want to buy it at that price because you don't believe the stock is worth it. Consequently, you have no problem not getting the stock that day.

When would you use day orders? It depends on your preferences and personal circumstances. I rarely use day orders because few events cause me to say, "Gee, I'll just try to buy or sell between now and the end of today's trading action." However, you may feel that you don't want a specified order to linger beyond today's market action. Perhaps you want to test a price. ("I want to get rid of stock A at $39 to make a quick profit, but it's currently trading at $37.50. However, I may change my mind tomorrow.") A day order is the perfect strategy to use in this case.

REMEMBER If you make a trade and don't specify a time limit with the order, most (if not all) brokers will automatically treat it as a day order.

Good-'til-canceled orders

A *GTC order* is the most commonly requested order by investors, and it's one that I use and recommend often. The GTC order means just what it says: The order stays in effect until it's transacted or until the investor cancels it. Although GTC orders are time related, they're always tied to a condition, such as the stock achieving a certain price.

Although the order implies that it can run indefinitely, most brokers have a limit of 30 or 60 days (or more). I've seen the limit as high as 120 days. By that time, the broker either cancels the order or contacts you (usually by email) to see whether you want to extend it. Ask your broker about their particular policy.

GTC orders are always coupled with condition-related orders (see the next section). For example, say you think that ASAP Corp. stock would make a good addition to your portfolio, but you don't want to buy it at the current price of $48 per share. You've done your homework on the stock, including looking at the stock's price-to-earnings ratio, price-to-book ratio, and so on (see Chapter 6 for more on ratios), and you say, "Hey, this stock isn't worth $48 a share. I'd only buy it at $36 per share." (It's over-priced or overvalued according to your analysis.) How should you proceed? Your best bet is to ask your broker to do a GTC order at $36. This request means that your broker will buy the shares if and when they hit the $36 mark (unless you cancel the order). Just make sure that your account has the funds available to complete the transaction.

GTC orders are very useful, so you should become familiar with your broker's policy on them. While you're at it, ask whether any fees apply. Many brokers don't charge for GTC orders because

REMEMBER if they happen to result in a buy (or sell) order, they generate a normal commission just as any stock transaction does. Other brokers may charge a small fee (but that's rare).

To be successful with GTC orders, you need to know the following:

>> **When you want to buy:** In recent years, people have had a tendency to rush into buying a stock without giving some thought to what they could do to get more for their money. Some investors don't realize that the stock market can be a place for bargain-hunting consumers. If you're ready to buy a quality pair of socks for $16 in a department store but the sales clerk says that those same socks are going on sale tomorrow for only $8, what do you do (assuming that you're a cost-conscious consumer)? Unless you're barefoot, you probably decide to wait. The same point holds true with stocks.

Say you want to buy SOX, Inc., at $26, but it's currently trading at $30. You think $30 is too expensive, but you'd be happy to buy the stock at $26 or lower. However, you have no idea whether the stock will move to your desired price today, tomorrow, next week, or even next month (or maybe never). In this case, a GTC order is appropriate.

>> **When you want to sell:** What if you buy some socks at a department store, and you discover that they have holes (darn it!)? Wouldn't you want to get rid of them? Of course you would. If a stock's price starts to unravel, you want to be able to get rid of it as well.

Perhaps you already own SOX at $25 but you're concerned that market conditions may drive the price lower. You're not sure which way the stock will move in the coming days and weeks. In this case, a GTC order to sell the stock at a specified price is a suitable strategy. Because the stock price is $25, you may want to place a GTC order to sell it if it falls to $22.50 in order to prevent further losses. Again, in this example, GTC is the time frame, and it accompanies a condition (sell when the stock hits $22.50).

Condition-related orders

A *condition-related order* (also known as a *conditional order*) is an order that's executed only when a certain condition is met.

Conditional orders enhance your ability to buy stocks at a lower price, to sell at a better price, or to minimize potential losses. When stock markets become bearish or uncertain, conditional orders are highly recommended.

A good example of a conditional order is a *limit order.* A limit order may say, "Buy Mojeski Corp. at $45." But if Mojeski Corp. isn't at $45 (this price is the condition), then the order isn't executed. I discuss limit orders, as well as market orders and stop-loss orders, in the following sections.

Market orders

When you buy stock, the simplest type of order is a *market order* — an order to buy or sell a stock at the market's current best available price. Orders don't get any more basic than that. Here's an example: Kowalski, Inc., is available at the market price of $10. When you call your broker and instruct them to buy 100 shares "at the market," the broker implements the order for your account, and you pay $1,000 plus commission.

WARNING

I say "current best available price" because the stock's price is constantly moving, and catching the best price can be a function of the broker's ability to process the stock purchase. For very active stocks, the price change can happen within seconds. It's not unheard of to have three brokers simultaneously place orders for the same stock and get three different prices because of differences in the brokers' capabilities. The difference may be pennies, but it's a difference nonetheless. (Some computers are faster than others.)

The advantage of a market order is that the transaction is processed immediately, and you get your stock without worrying about whether it hits a particular price. For example, if you buy Kowalski, Inc., with a market order, you know that by the end of that phone call (or website visit), you're assured of getting the stock. The disadvantage of a market order is that you can't control the price at which you purchase the stock. Whether you're buying or selling your shares, you may not realize the exact price you expect (especially if you're dealing with a volatile stock).

REMEMBER

Market orders get finalized in the chronological order in which they're placed. Your price may change because the orders ahead of you in line cause the stock price to rise or fall based on the latest news.

Stop-loss orders

A *stop-loss order* (also called a *stop order*) is a condition-related order that instructs the broker to sell a particular stock in your portfolio only when the stock reaches a particular price. It acts like a trigger, and the stop order converts to a market order to sell the stock immediately.

REMEMBER

The stop-loss order isn't designed to take advantage of small, short-term moves in the stock's price. It's meant to help you protect the bulk of your money when the market turns against your stock investment in a sudden manner.

Say your Kowalski, Inc., stock rises to $20 per share, and you seek to protect your investment against a possible future market decline. A stop-loss order at $18 triggers your broker to sell the stock immediately if it falls to the $18 mark. In this example, if the stock suddenly drops to $17, it still triggers the stop-loss order, but the finalized sale price is $17. In a volatile market, you may not be able to sell at your precise stop-loss price. However, because the order automatically gets converted into a market order, the sale will be done, and you'll be spared further declines in the stock.

The main benefit of a stop-loss order is that it prevents a major loss in a stock that you own. It's a form of discipline that's important in investing to minimize potential losses. Investors can find it agonizing to sell a stock that has fallen. If they don't sell, however, the stock often continues to plummet as investors continue to hold on while hoping for a rebound in the price.

TIP

Most investors set a stop-loss amount at about 10 percent below the market value of the stock. This percentage gives the stock some room to fluctuate, which most stocks tend to do from day to day. If you're extra nervous, consider a tighter stop-loss amount, such as 5 percent or less.

Keep in mind that this order only triggers the sale, and a particular price isn't guaranteed to be captured because the actual buy or sell occurs immediately after the trigger is activated. If the market at the time of the actual transaction is particularly volatile, then the price realized may be significantly different.

In the following sections, I describe a certain type of stop-loss order (called a trailing stop), and I talk about the use of beta measurement with stop-loss orders.

TRAILING STOPS

Trailing stops are an important technique in wealth preservation for seasoned stock investors and can be one of your key strategies in using stop-loss orders. A *trailing stop* is a stop-loss order that an investor actively manages by moving it up along with the stock's market price. The stop-loss order "trails" the stock price upward. As the stop-loss goes upward, it protects more and more of the stock's value from declining.

Imagine that you bought stock in Peach, Inc., for $30 a share. A trailing stop is in place at, say, 10 percent, and the order is GTC (presume that this broker places a time limit of 90 days for GTC orders). At $30 per share, the trailing stop is $27. If Peach goes to $40, your trailing stop automatically rises to $36. If Peach continues to rise to $50, your trailing continues along with it to $45. Now say that Peach reverses course (for whatever reason) and starts to plummet. The trailing stop stays put at $45 and triggers a sell order if Peach reaches the $45 level.

In the preceding example, I use a trailing-stop percentage, but trailing stops are also available in dollar amounts. For example, say Peach is at $30, and I put in a trailing stop of $3. If Peach rises to $50, my trailing stop will reach $47. If Peach then drops from this peak of $50, the trailing stop stays put at $47 and triggers a sell order if Peach actually hits $47. You get the picture. Trailing stops can help you sleep at night, especially in these turbulent times.

William O'Neill, founder and publisher of *Investor's Business Daily*, advocates setting a trailing stop of 8 percent below your purchase price. That's his preference. Some investors who invest in very volatile stocks may put in trailing stops of 20 percent or 25 percent. Is a stop-loss order desirable or advisable in every situation? No. It depends on your level of experience, your investment goals, and the market environment. Still, stop-loss orders (trailing or otherwise) are appropriate in many cases, especially if the market seems uncertain (or you are!).

A trailing stop is a stop-loss order that you actively manage. The stop-loss order is GTC, and it constantly trails the stock's price as it moves up. To successfully implement stop-loss orders (including trailing stops), you should

>> **Realize that brokers usually don't place trailing stops for you automatically.** In fact, they won't (or shouldn't) place any type of order without your consent. Deciding on the type of order to place is your responsibility. You can raise, lower, or cancel a trailing-stop order at will, but you need to monitor your investment when substantial moves do occur to respond to the movement appropriately.

>> **Change the stop-loss order when the stock price moves significantly.** Hopefully, you won't call your broker every time the stock moves 50 cents. Change the stop-loss order when the stock price moves around 10 percent. For example, if you initially purchase a stock at $90 per share, ask the broker to place the stop-loss order at $81. When the stock moves to $100, cancel the $81 stop-loss order and replace it at $90. When the stock's price moves to $110, change the stop-loss order to $99, and so on.

>> **Understand your broker's policy on GTC orders.** If your broker usually considers a GTC order expired after 30 or 60 days, you should be aware of it. You don't want to risk a sudden drop in your stock's price without the stop-loss order protection. Make a note of your broker's time limit so you remember to renew the order for additional time.

>> **Monitor your stock.** A trailing stop isn't a "set it and forget it" technique. Monitoring your investment is critical. Of course, if the investment falls, the stop-loss order prevents further loss. If the stock price rises substantially, remember to adjust your trailing stop accordingly. Keep raising the safety net as the stock continues to rise. Part of monitoring the stock is knowing the beta, which you can read more about in the next section.

BETA MEASUREMENT

To be a successful investor, you need to understand the volatility of the particular stock you invest in. In stock-market parlance, this volatility is also called the beta of a stock. *Beta* is a quantitative measure of the volatility of a given stock (mutual funds and portfolios, too) relative to the overall market, usually the S&P 500 (see Chapter 11). Beta specifically measures the performance movement of the stock as the S&P moves 1 percent up or down. A beta measurement above 1 is more volatile than the overall market, whereas a beta below 1 is less volatile. Some stocks are relatively stable in terms of price movements; others jump around.

Because beta measures how volatile or unstable the stock's price is, it tends to be uttered in the same breath as *risk* — more volatility indicates more risk. Similarly, less volatility tends to mean less risk. (Chapter 4 offers more details on the topics of risk and volatility.)

TIP

You can find a company's beta at websites that provide a lot of financial information about companies, such as Nasdaq (www.nasdaq.com), Investing.com (www.investing.com), or Yahoo! Finance (https://finance.yahoo.com).

The beta is useful to know when it comes to stop-loss orders because it gives you a general idea of the stock's trading range. If a stock is currently priced at $50 and it typically trades in the $48 to $52 range, then a trailing stop at $49 doesn't make sense. Your stock would probably be sold the same day you initiated the stop-loss order. If your stock is a volatile growth stock that may swing up and down by 10 percent, you should more logically set your stop-loss at 15 percent below that day's price.

REMEMBER

The stock of a large-cap company in a mature industry tends to have a low beta — one close to the overall market. Small- and mid-cap stocks in new or emerging industries tend to have greater volatility in their day-to-day price fluctuations; hence, they tend to have a high beta. (You can find out more about large-, small-, and mid-cap stocks in Chapter 1; Chapter 4 has more about beta.)

Limit orders

A *limit order* is a very precise condition-related order implying that a limit exists either on the buy side or the sell side of the transaction. You want to buy (or sell) only at a specified price. Period. Limit orders work well if you're buying the stock, but they may not be good for you if you're selling the stock. Here's how they work in both instances:

>> **When you're buying:** Just because you like a particular company and you want its stock doesn't mean that you're willing to pay the current market price. Maybe you want to buy Kowalski, Inc., but the current market price of $20 per share isn't acceptable to you. You prefer to buy it at $16 because you think that price reflects its true market value. What do you do? You tell your broker, "Buy Kowalski with a limit order at $16" (or you can enter a limit order at the broker's website). You have to specify whether it's a day order or a GTC order, both of which I discuss earlier in this chapter.

What happens if the stock experiences great volatility? What if it drops to $16.01 and then suddenly drops to $15.95 on the next move? Nothing happens, actually, which you may be dismayed to hear. Because your order was limited to $16, it can be transacted only at $16 — no more and no less. The only way for this particular trade to occur is if the stock rises back to $16. However, if the price keeps dropping, your limit order isn't transacted and may expire or be canceled.

WARNING

>> **When you're selling:** Limit orders are activated only when a stock hits a specific price. If you buy Kowalski, Inc., at $20 and you worry about a decline in the share price, you may decide to put in a limit order at $18. If you watch the news and hear that Kowalski's price is dropping, you may sigh and say, "I sure am glad I put in that limit order at $18!" However, in a volatile market, the share price may leapfrog over your specified price. It could go from $18.01 to $17.99 and then continue its descent. Because the stock price never hit $18 on the mark, your stock isn't sold. You may be sitting at home satisfied (mistakenly) that you played it smart, while your stock plummets to $15, $10, or worse! Having a stop-loss order in place is best.

Investors who aren't in a hurry can use a limit order to try to get a better price when they decide to sell. For example, maybe you own a stock whose price is at $50 and you want to sell, but you think that a short-term rally in the stock is imminent. In that case, you can use a limit order such as "Sell the stock at the sell limit order of $55, and keep the order on for 30 days."

When you're buying (or selling) a stock, most brokers interpret the limit order as "buy (or sell) at this specific price or better." For example, presumably, if your limit order is to buy a stock at $10, you'll be just as happy if your broker buys that stock at $9.95. That way, if you don't get exactly $10 because the stock's price was volatile, you'll still get the stock at a lower price. Talk to your broker to be clear on the meaning of the limit order.

Advanced orders

Brokers have added sophisticated capabilities to the existing repertoire of orders that are available for stock investors. One example is *advanced orders*, which provide investors with a way to use a combination of orders for more sophisticated trades. An example of an advanced order is something like, "Only sell stock B, and if it sells, use the proceeds to buy stock D." You get the idea. My brokerage firm has the following on its website, and I'm sure that more firms will do the same. Inquire with yours and see the benefit of using advanced orders such as the following:

» **"One order cancels another order":** In this scenario you enter two orders simultaneously with the condition that if one order is executed, the second order is automatically canceled.

» **"One order triggers another order":** Here you submit an order, and if that order is filled, another order is automatically submitted. Many brokers have different names for these types of orders, so ask them whether they can provide such an order.

TIP

Other types of advanced orders and order strategies are available, but you get the picture. Talk to your brokerage firm, and find out what's available in your particular account.

Buying on Margin

Buying on margin means buying securities, such as stocks, with funds you borrow from your broker. Buying stock on margin is similar to buying a house with a mortgage. If you buy a house at a purchase price of $100,000 and put 10 percent down, your *equity* (the part you own) is $10,000, and you borrow the remaining $90,000 with a mortgage. If the value of the house rises to $120,000 and you sell (for the sake of simplicity, I won't include closing costs in this example), you make a profit of 200 percent. How is that? The $20,000 gain on the property represents a gain of 20 percent on the purchase price of $100,000, but because your real investment is $10,000 (the down payment), your gain works out to 200 percent (a gain of $20,000 on your initial investment of $10,000).

WARNING

Buying on margin is an example of using leverage to maximize your gain when prices rise. *Leverage* is simply using borrowed money when you make an asset purchase to increase your potential profit. This type of leverage is great in a favorable (bull) market, but it works against you in an unfavorable (bear) market. Say a $100,000 house you purchase with a $90,000 mortgage falls in value to $80,000 (and property values can decrease during economic hard times). Your outstanding debt of $90,000 exceeds the value of the property. Because you owe more than you own, you're left with a negative net worth.

REMEMBER

Leverage is a double-edged sword. Don't forget that you need approval from your brokerage firm before you can buy on margin. To buy on margin, you typically fill out the form provided by that brokerage firm to be approved. Keep in mind that brokers typically require accounts to have a minimum of $2,000 or more before the investor can be approved for margin. Check with your broker because each firm has different requirements.

In the following sections, I describe the potential outcomes of buying on margin, explain how to maintain a balance, and provide some pointers for successfully buying on margin.

Examining marginal outcomes

Suppose you think that the stock for the company Murgatroyd, Inc., currently at $40 per share, will go up in value. You want to buy 100 shares, but you have only $2,000. What can you do? If you're intent on buying 100 shares (versus simply buying the 50 shares that you have cash for), you can borrow the additional $2,000 from your broker on margin. If you do that, what are the potential outcomes?

If the stock price goes up

This outcome is the best for you. If Murgatroyd goes to $50 per share, your investment is worth $5,000, and your outstanding margin loan is $2,000. If you sell, the total proceeds will pay off the loan and leave you with $3,000. Because your initial investment was $2,000, your profit is a solid 50 percent because your $2,000 principal amount generated a $1,000 profit. (For the sake of this example, I leave out any charges, such as commissions and interest paid on the margin loan.) However, if you pay the entire $4,000 up front without the margin loan, your $4,000 investment generates a profit of $1,000, or 25 percent. Using margin, you double the return on your money.

Leverage, when used properly, is very profitable. However, it's still debt, so understand that you must pay it off eventually, regardless of the stock's performance.

If the stock price fails to rise

If the stock goes nowhere, you still have to pay interest on that margin loan. If the stock pays dividends, this money can defray some of the margin loan's cost. In other words, dividends can help you pay off what you borrow from the broker. (Chapter 3 provides an introduction to dividends, and Chapter 10 covers dividend-investing and other income strategies.)

Having the stock neither rise nor fall may seem like a neutral situation, but you pay interest on your margin loan with each passing day. For this reason, margin trading can be a good consideration for conservative investors if the stock pays a high dividend. Many times, a high dividend from $4,000 of stock can equal or exceed the margin interest you have to pay from the $2,000 (50 percent) you borrow from the broker to buy that stock.

If the stock price goes down, buying on margin can work against you. What if Murgatroyd goes to $38 per share? The market value of 100 shares is then $3,800, but your equity shrinks to only $1,800 because you have to pay your $2,000 margin loan. You're not exactly looking at a disaster at this point, but you'd better be careful, because the margin loan exceeds 50 percent of your stock investment. If it goes any lower, you may get the dreaded *margin call*, when the broker actually contacts you to ask you to restore the ratio between the margin loan and the value of the securities. (See the next section for information about appropriate debt-to-equity ratios.)

Maintaining your balance

When you purchase stock on margin, you must maintain a balanced ratio of margin debt to equity of at least 50 percent. If the debt portion exceeds this limit, you're required to restore that ratio by depositing either more stock or more cash into your brokerage account. The additional stock you deposit can be stock that's transferred from another account.

To continue the example from the previous section: If Murgatroyd goes to $28 per share, the margin-loan portion exceeds 50 percent of the equity value in that stock — in this case, because the market value of your stock is $2,800 but the margin loan is still at $2,000, the margin loan is a worrisome 71 percent of the market value ($2,000 ÷ $2,800 = 71 percent). Expect to get a call from your broker to put more securities or cash into the account to restore the 50 percent balance.

If you can't come up with more stock, other securities, or cash, the next step is to sell stock from the account and use the proceeds to pay off the margin loan. For you, that means realizing a capital loss — you lose money on your investment.

TIP

The Federal Reserve Board governs margin requirements for brokers with Regulation T. Discuss this rule with your broker to understand fully your (and the broker's) risks and obligations. Regulation T dictates margin requirements set by brokers for their customers. For most listed stocks, it's 50 percent.

Striving for success on margin

Margin, as you can see from the previous sections, can escalate your profits on the upside but magnify your losses on the downside. If your stock plummets drastically, you can end up with a margin loan that exceeds the market value of the stock you used the loan to purchase. In December 2018, one of the worst months in recent memory, excessive exposure of margin debt exacerbated the losses as many investors were forced to sell and pay back the margin debt. Ugh!

WARNING

If you buy stock on margin, use a disciplined approach. Be extra careful when using leverage, such as a margin loan, because it can backfire. Keep the following points in mind:

- >> **Have ample reserves of cash or marginable securities in your account.** Try to keep the margin ratio at 40 percent or less to minimize the chance of a margin call.

- >> **If you're a beginner, consider using margin to buy stocks in large companies that have relatively stable prices and pay good dividends.** Some people buy income stocks that have dividend yields that exceed the margin interest rate, meaning that the stock ends up paying for its own margin loan. Just remember those stop-loss orders, which I discuss earlier in this chapter.

- >> **Constantly monitor your stocks.** If the market turns against you, the result will be especially painful if you use margin.

- >> **Have a payback plan for your margin debt.** Taking margin loans against your investments means that you're paying interest. Your ultimate goal is to make money, and paying interest eats into your profits.

Going Short and Coming Out Ahead

The vast majority of stock investors are familiar with buying stock, holding onto it for a while, and hoping its value goes up. This kind of thinking is called *going long*, and investors who go long are considered to be *long on stocks*. Going long essentially means that you're bullish and seeking your profits from rising prices. However, astute investors also profit in the market when stock prices fall. *Going short* on a stock (also called *shorting a stock, selling short,* or *doing a short sale*) is a common technique for profiting from a stock price decline. Investors have made big profits during bear markets by going short. A short sale is a bet that a particular stock is going down.

Most people easily understand making money by going long. It boils down to "buy low and sell high." Piece of cake. Going short means making money by selling high and then buying low. Huh? Thinking in reverse isn't a piece of cake. Although thinking of this stock adage in reverse may be challenging, the mechanics of going short are really simple. Consider an example that uses a fictitious company called DOA, Inc. As a stock, DOA ($50 per share) is looking pretty sickly. It has lots of debt and plummeting sales and earnings, and the news is out that DOA's industry will face hard times for the foreseeable future. This situation describes a stock that's an ideal candidate for shorting. The future may be bleak for DOA, but it's promising for savvy investors. The following sections provide the full scoop on going short.

To go short, you have to be deemed (by your broker) creditworthy — your account needs to be approved for short selling. When you're approved for margin trading, you're probably set to sell short, too. Talk to your broker (or check the broker's website for information) about limitations in your account regarding going short.

You must understand brokerage rules before you conduct short selling. Your broker must approve you for it (see Chapter 8 for information on working with brokers), and you must meet the minimum collateral requirement, which is typically $2,000 or 50 percent (whichever is higher) of the shorted stock's market value. If the stock generates dividends, those dividends are paid to the stock's owner, not to the person who borrows to go short. Check with your broker for complete details.

Because going short on stocks has greater risks than going long, I strongly advise beginning investors to avoid shorting stocks until they become more seasoned.

Setting up a short sale

This section explains how to go short. Say you believe DOA is the right stock to short — you're pretty sure its price is going to fall. With DOA at $50, you instruct your broker to "go short 100 shares on DOA." (It doesn't have to be 100 shares; I'm just using that as an example.) Here's what happens next:

1. **Your broker borrows 100 shares of DOA stock, either from their own inventory or from another client or broker.**

   That's right. The stock can be borrowed from a client, no permission necessary. The broker guarantees the transaction, and the client/stock owner never has to be informed about it because they never lose legal and beneficial right to the stock. You borrow 100 shares, and you'll return 100 shares when it's time to complete the transaction.

2. **Your broker sells the stock and puts the money in your account.**

   Your account is credited with $5,000 (100 shares × $50 per share) in cash — the money gained from selling the borrowed stock. This cash acts like a loan on which you're going to have to pay interest.

3. **You buy the stock back and return it to its rightful owner.**

   When it's time to close the transaction (either because you want to close it or because the owner of the shares wants to sell them, so you have to give them back), you must return the number of shares you borrowed (in this case, 100 shares). If you buy back the 100 shares at $40 per share (remember that you shorted this particular stock because you were sure its price was going to fall) and those 100 shares are returned to their owner, you make a $1,000 profit. (To keep the example tidy, I'm not including brokerage commissions.)

Oops! Going short when prices grow taller

I bet you guessed that the wonderful profitability of selling short has a flip side. Say you were wrong about DOA and the stock price rises from the ashes as it goes from $50 to $87. Now what? You still have to return the 100 shares you borrowed. With the stock's price at $87, that means you have to buy the stock for $8,700 (100 shares at the new, higher price of $87). Ouch! How do you pay for it? Well, you have that original $5,000 in your account from when you initially went short on the stock. But where do you get the other $3,700 ($8,700 less the original $5,000)? You guessed it — your pocket! You have to cough up the difference. If the stock continues to rise, that's a lot of coughing.

WARNING

How much money do you lose if the stock goes to $100 or more? A heck of a lot. As a matter of fact, there's no limit to how much you can lose. That's why going short can be riskier than going long. When going long, the most you can lose is 100 percent of your money. When you go short, however, you can lose more than 100 percent of the money you invest. Yikes!

TIP

Because the potential for loss is unlimited when you short a stock, I suggest that you use a stop order (also called a *buy-stop order*) to minimize the damage. Better yet, make it a GTC order, which I discuss earlier in this chapter. You can set the stop order at a given price, and if the stock hits that price, you buy the stock back so you can return it to its owner before the price rises even higher. You still lose money, but you limit your losses. Like a stop-loss order, a buy-stop order effectively works to limit your loss.

Feeling the squeeze

If you go short on a stock, you have to buy that stock back sooner or later so you can return it to its owner. What happens when a lot of people are short on a particular stock and its price starts to rise? All those short sellers are scrambling to buy the stock back so that they can close their transactions before they lose too much money. This mass buying quickens the pace of the stock's ascent and puts a squeeze (called a *short squeeze*) on the investors who've been shorting the stock.

In the earlier section "Setting up a short sale," I explain that your broker can borrow stock from another client so you can go short on it. What happens when that client wants to sell the stock in their account — the stock that you borrowed and that is, therefore, no longer in their account? When that happens, your broker asks you to return the borrowed stock. That's when you feel the squeeze — you have to buy the stock back at the current price.

WARNING

Going short can be a great maneuver in a declining (bear) market, but it can be brutal if the stock price goes up. If you're a beginner, stay away from short selling until you have enough experience (and money) to risk it.

Chapter **14**

Handling Taxes on Stock Investments

After conquering the world of making money with stocks, now you have another hurdle: keeping your hard-earned money! Some people may tell you that taxes are brutal, complicated, and counterproductive; others may tell you that they're a form of legalized thievery; and still others may say that they're a necessary evil. And then there are the pessimists. In any case, this chapter shows you how to keep more of the fruits from your hard-earned labor.

REMEMBER

Keep in mind that this chapter isn't meant to be comprehensive. For a fuller treatment of personal taxes, you should check with your personal tax advisor and get the publications referenced in this chapter by visiting the Internal Revenue Service (IRS) website at www.irs.gov or calling the IRS publications department at 800-829-3676.

However, in this chapter, I cover the most relevant points for stock investors, such as the tax treatment for dividends and capital gains and losses, common tax deductions for investors, some simple tax-reduction strategies, and pointers for retirement investing. And yes, I cover these points through the lens of recent tax law changes.

Tax laws can be very hairy and perplexing, and you can easily feel like the mouse going through the maze trying to find the cheese (a tax refund) or just keep more of the hard-earned cheese you took home. Higher (and more complicated) taxes generally aren't good for stock investors or the economy at large, but fortunately recent tax laws do have some good news for most investors. But no matter how friendly or unfriendly the tax environment is, you should stay informed through your tax advisor, online tax information sources, and taxpayer advocacy groups like the National Taxpayers Union (www.ntu.org). 'Nuff said.

The IRS will usually put the more current up-and-coming changes and updates at www.irs.gov/newsroom. It's a service of the IRS's Taxpayer Advocate Service (www.taxpayeradvocate.irs.gov). It shows you the tax changes for 2022, 2023, and subsequent tax years. It also shows you what changes have occurred either by looking at the actual line items on Form 1040 or by topic or sub-topic. It even shows you how to calculate your paycheck's withholdings so you can more closely match the withholdings to the new potential tax rates to avoid under- or overwithholding.

Paying Up: The Tax Treatment of Different Stock Investments

The following sections tell you what you need to know about the tax implications you face when you start investing in stocks. It's good to know in advance the basics on ordinary income, capital gains, and capital losses because they may affect your investing strategy and your long-term wealth-building plans.

Understanding ordinary income and capital gains

Profit you make from your stock investments can be taxed in one of two ways, depending on the type of profit:

>> **Ordinary income:** Your profit can be taxed at the same rate as wages or interest — at your full, regular tax rate. If your tax bracket is 28 percent, for example, that's the rate at which your ordinary income investment profit is taxed. Two types of investment profits get taxed as ordinary income:

- **Dividends:** When you receive dividends (either in cash or stock), they're taxed as ordinary income. This is true even if those dividends are in a dividend reinvestment plan. If, however, the dividends occur in a tax-sheltered plan, such as an individual retirement account (IRA) or 401(k) plan, then they're exempt from taxes for as long as they're in the plan. (Retirement plans are covered in the later section "Using Tax-Advantaged Retirement Investing.")

  Keep in mind that qualified dividends are taxed at a lower rate than nonqualified dividends. A *qualified dividend* is a dividend that receives preferential tax treatment versus other types of dividends, such as unqualified dividends or interest. Typically a dividend is qualified if it is issued by a U.S. corporation (or a foreign corporation listed on U.S. stock exchanges), and the stock is held longer than 60 days. An example of an ordinary dividend that is not qualified is a dividend paid out by a money-market fund or a bond-related exchange-traded fund (ETF), because the dividend is technically interest.

- **Short-term capital gains:** If you sell stock for a gain and you've owned the stock for one year or less, the gain is considered ordinary income. To calculate the time, you use the *trade date* (or *date of execution*). This is the date on which you executed the order, not the settlement date. (For more on important dates, see Chapter 5.) However, if these gains occur in a tax-sheltered plan, such as a 401(k) or an IRA, no tax is triggered.

Check out IRS Publication 550, "Investment Income and Expenses," for more information.

>> **Long-term capital gains:** These are usually much better for you than ordinary income or short-term gains as far as taxes are concerned. The tax laws reward patient investors. After you've held the stock for at least a year and a day (what a difference a day makes!), your tax rate on that gain may be lower. (See the next section for more specifics on potential savings.) Get more information on capital gains in IRS Publication 550. Fortunately, you can time stock sales, so always consider pushing back the sale date (if possible) to take advantage of the lesser capital gains tax.

You can control how you manage the tax burden from your investment profits. Gains are taxable only if a sale actually takes place (in other words, only if the gain is *realized*). If your stock in GazillionBucks, Inc., goes from $5 per share to $87 per share, that $82 appreciation isn't subject to taxation unless you actually sell the stock. Until you sell, that gain is *unrealized.* To minimize the amount of taxes you have to pay on stock sales, time them carefully and hold onto stocks for at least a year and a day (to make the gains long term).

When you buy stock, record the date of purchase and the *cost basis* (the purchase price of the stock plus any ancillary charges, such as commissions). This information will be very important come tax time if you decide to sell your stock. The date of purchase (also known as the *date of execution*) helps establish the *holding period* (how long you own the stocks) that determines whether your gains are considered short term or long term.

Say you buy 100 shares of GazillionBucks, Inc., at $5 and pay a commission of $8. Your cost basis is $508 (100 shares × $5 + $8 commission). If you sell the stock at $87 per share and pay a $12 commission, the total sale amount is $8,688 (100 shares × $87 – $12 commission). If this sale occurs less than a year after the purchase, it's a short-term gain. In the 28 percent tax bracket, the short-term gain of $8,180 ($8,688 – $508) is also taxed at 28 percent. Read the following section to see the tax implications if your gain is a long-term gain.

Any gain (or loss) from a short sale is considered short term regardless of how long the position is held open. (For more information on the mechanics of selling short, check out Chapter 13.)

Minimizing the tax on your capital gains

Long-term capital gains are taxed at a more favorable rate than ordinary income. To qualify for long-term capital gains treatment, you must hold the investment for more than one year (in other words, for at least one year and one day).

Recall the example in the preceding section with GazillionBucks, Inc. As a short-term transaction at the 28 percent tax rate, the tax is $2,290 ($8,180 × 28 percent). After you revive, you say, "Gasp!

What a chunk of dough. I'd better hold off a while longer." You hold onto the stock for more than a year to achieve the status of long-term capital gains. How does that change the tax? For anyone in the 28 percent tax bracket or higher, the long-term capital gains rate of 15 percent applies. In this case, the tax is $1,227 ($8,180 × 15 percent), resulting in a tax savings to you of $1,063 ($2,290 − $1,227). Okay, it's not a fortune, but it's a substantial difference from the original tax. After all, successful stock investing isn't only about making money; it's about keeping it, too.

Capital gains taxes *can* be lower than the tax on ordinary income, but they aren't higher. If, for example, you're in the 15 percent tax bracket for ordinary income and you have a long-term capital gain that would normally bump you up to the 28 percent tax bracket, the gain is taxed at your lower rate of 15 percent instead of a higher capital gains rate. Check with your tax advisor on a regular basis because this rule could change due to new tax laws.

REMEMBER

Don't sell a stock just because it qualifies for long-term capital gains treatment, even if the sale eases your tax burden. If the stock is doing well and meets your investing criteria, hold onto it.

DEBT AND TAXES: ANOTHER ANGLE

If you truly need cash but you don't want to sell your stock because it's doing well, and you want to avoid paying capital gains tax, consider borrowing against it. If the stock is listed (on the New York Stock Exchange, for example) and is in a brokerage account with margin privileges, you can borrow up to 50 percent of the value of marginable securities at favorable rates (listed stocks are marginable securities). The money you borrow is considered a margin loan (see Chapter 13), and the interest you pay is low (compared to credit cards or personal loans) because it's considered a secured loan (your stock acts as collateral).

On those rare occasions when I use margin, I usually make sure I use stocks that generate a high dividend. That way, the stocks themselves help pay off the margin loan. In addition, if the proceeds are used for an investment purpose, the margin interest may be tax-deductible. See IRS Publication 550 for more details.

Coping with capital losses

Ever think that having the value of your stocks fall could be a good thing? Perhaps the only real positive regarding losses in your portfolio is that they can reduce your taxes. A *capital loss* means that you lost money on your investments. This amount is generally deductible on your tax return, and you can claim a loss on either long-term or short-term stock holdings. This loss can go against your other income and lower your overall tax.

Say you bought Worth Zilch Co. stock for a total purchase price of $3,500 and sold it later at a sale price of $800. Your tax-deductible capital loss is $2,700.

REMEMBER

The one string attached to deducting investment losses on your tax return is that the most you can report in a single year is $3,000. On the bright side, though, any excess loss isn't really lost — you can carry it forward to the next year. If you have net investment losses of $4,500 in 2022, you can deduct $3,000 in 2022, carry the remaining $1,500 loss over to 2023, and deduct the loss on your 2023 tax return. That $1,500 loss may then offset any gains you're looking to realize in 2023.

Before you can deduct losses, you must first use them to offset any capital gains. If you realize long-term capital gains of $7,000 in Stock A and long-term capital losses of $6,000 in Stock B, you have a net long-term capital gain of $1,000 ($7,000 gain minus the offset of $6,000 loss). Whenever possible, see whether losses in your portfolio can be realized to offset any capital gains to reduce potential tax. IRS Publication 550 includes information for investors on capital gains and losses.

TIP

Here's your optimum strategy: Where possible, keep losses on a short-term basis, and push your gains into long-term capital gains status. If a transaction can't be tax-free, at the very least try to defer the tax to keep your money working for you.

Evaluating gains and losses scenarios

Of course, any investor can come up with hundreds of possible gains and losses scenarios. For example, you may wonder what happens if you sell part of your holdings now as a short-term capital loss and the remainder later as a long-term capital gain. You must look at each sale of stock (or potential sale) methodically to calculate the gain or loss you would realize from it. Figuring out your gain or loss isn't that complicated. Here are some general rules to help you wade through the morass. If you add up all your gains and losses and

>> **The net result is a short-term gain:** It's taxed at your highest tax bracket (as ordinary income).

>> **The net result is a long-term gain:** It's taxed at 15 percent if you're in the 28 percent tax bracket or higher. Check with your tax advisor on changes here that may affect your taxes.

>> **The net result is a loss of $3,000 or less:** It's fully deductible against other income. If you're married filing separately, your deduction limit is $1,500.

>> **The net result is a loss that exceeds $3,000:** You can only deduct up to $3,000 in that year; the remainder goes forward to future years.

Sharing Your Gains with the IRS

Of course, you don't want to pay more taxes than you have to, but as the old cliché goes, "Don't let the tax tail wag the investment dog." You should buy or sell a stock because it makes economic sense first, and *then* consider the tax implications. After all, taxes consume a relatively small portion of your gain. As long as you experience a *net gain* (gain after all transaction costs, including taxes, brokerage fees, and other related fees), consider yourself a successful investor — even if you have to give away some of your gain to taxes.

TIP

Try to make tax planning second nature in your day-to-day activities. No, you don't have to consume yourself with a blizzard of paperwork and tax projections. I simply mean that when you make a stock transaction, keep the receipt and order confirmation and maintain good records. When you're considering a large purchase or sale, pause for a moment, and ask yourself whether this transaction will have positive or negative tax consequences. (Refer to the earlier section "Paying Up: The Tax Treatment of Different Stock Investments" to review various tax scenarios.) Speak to a tax consultant beforehand to discuss the ramifications.

In the following sections, I describe the tax forms you need to fill out, as well as some important rules to follow.

Filling out forms

Most investors report their investment-related activities on their individual tax returns (Form 1040). The reports that you'll likely receive from brokers and other investment sources include the following:

>> **Brokerage and bank statements:** Monthly statements that you receive

>> **Trade confirmations:** Documents to confirm that you bought or sold stock

>> **1099-DIV:** Reporting dividends paid to you

>> **1099-INT:** Reporting interest paid to you

>> **1099-B:** Reporting gross proceeds submitted to you from the sale of investments, such as stocks and mutual funds

You may receive other, more obscure forms that aren't listed here. You should retain all documents related to your stock investments.

REMEMBER   The IRS schedules and forms that most stock investors need to be aware of and/or attach to their Form 1040 include the following:

>> **Schedule B:** To report interest and dividends

>> **Schedule D:** To report capital gains and losses

>> **Form 4952:** To calculate the amount of investment interest expense you can deduct this year and carry forward to future years

>> **Publication 17:** For use in preparing your tax return

You can get these publications directly from the IRS at 800-829-3676, or you can download them from the website (www.irs.gov). For more information on what records and documentation investors should hang onto, check out IRS Publication 552, "Recordkeeping for Individuals."

If you plan to do your own taxes, consider using the latest tax software products, which are inexpensive and easy to use. These programs usually have a question-and-answer feature to help you do your taxes step-by-step, and they include all the necessary

TIP

forms. Consider getting either TurboTax (https://turbotax.intuit.com) or H&R Block (www.hrblock.com/tax-software). Alternatively, you can get free tax preparation software at www.taxact.com.

Playing by the rules

WARNING

Some people get the smart idea of "Hey! Why not sell my losing stock by December 31 to grab the short-term loss and just buy back the stock on January 2 so I can have my cake and eat it, too?" Not so fast. The IRS put the kibosh on maneuvers like that with something called the *wash-sale rule.* This rule states that if you sell a stock for a loss and buy it back within 30 days, the loss isn't valid because you didn't make any substantial investment change. The wash-sale rule applies only to losses. The way around the rule is simple: Wait at least 31 days before you buy that identical stock back again.

Some people try to get around the wash-sale rule by doubling up on their stock position with the intention of selling half. Therefore, the IRS makes the 30-day rule cover both sides of the sale date. That way, an investor can't buy the identical stock within 30 days just before the sale and then realize a short-term loss for tax purposes.

Discovering the Softer Side of the IRS: Tax Deductions for Investors

In the course of managing your portfolio of stocks and other investments, you'll probably incur expenses that are tax-deductible. The tax laws allow you to write off certain investment-related expenses as itemized expenses on Schedule A, an attachment to IRS Form 1040. Keep records of your deductions and retain a checklist to remind you which deductions you normally take. IRS Publication 550 ("Investment Income and Expenses") gives you more details.

The following sections explain common tax deductions for investors: investment interest, miscellaneous expenses, and donations to charity. I also list a few items you *can't* deduct.

Keep in mind that the standard deduction for individuals has increased significantly, so you may not need to itemize on Schedule A because the standard deduction will give many folks a greater tax benefit. For 2023, the standard deduction for those married filing jointly is $27,700 (in 2022, it was $25,900). Because the 2018 tax act made the standard deduction significantly higher (in 2017, it was only $12,700 for married filing jointly), itemizing (using Schedule A) was less attractive — total itemized deductions needed to be at a higher total than the standard deduction before itemizing made tax sense. The issue for stock investors is that many investment-related deductible expenses are claimed as itemized (Schedule A) expenses, so it will be more difficult to clear the hurdle of the new, higher standard deduction.

Investment interest

If you pay any interest to a stockbroker, such as margin interest or any interest to acquire a taxable financial investment, that's considered investment interest and is usually fully deductible as an itemized expense.

Keep in mind that not all interest is deductible. Consumer interest or interest paid for any consumer or personal purpose isn't deductible. For more general information, see the section covering interest in IRS Publication 17.

Miscellaneous expenses

Most investment-related deductions are reported as miscellaneous expenses. Here are some common deductions:

» Accounting or bookkeeping fees for keeping records of investment income

» Any expense related to tax service, tax programs, or tax education

» Computer expense — you can take a depreciation deduction for your computer if you use it 50 percent of the time or more for managing your investments

» Investment management or investment advisor's fees (fees paid for advice on tax-exempt investments aren't deductible)

» Legal fees involving stockholder issues

>> Safe-deposit box rental fee or home safe to hold your securities, unless used to hold personal effects or tax-exempt securities

>> Service charges for collecting interest and dividends

>> Subscription fees for investment advisory services

>> Travel costs to check investments or to confer with advisors regarding income-related investments

REMEMBER

You can deduct only that portion of your miscellaneous expenses that exceeds 2 percent of your adjusted gross income. For more information on deducting miscellaneous expenses, check out IRS Publication 529.

Donations of stock to charity

What happens if you donate stock to your favorite (IRS-approved) charity? Because it's a noncash charitable contribution, you can deduct the market value of the stock.

Say that last year you bought stock for $2,000 and it's worth $4,000 this year. If you donate it this year, you can write off the market value at the time of the contribution. In this case, you have a $4,000 deduction. Use IRS Form 8283, which is an attachment to Schedule A, to report noncash contributions exceeding $500.

TIP

To get more guidance from the IRS on this matter, get Publication 526, "Charitable Contributions."

Items that you can't deduct

WARNING

Just to be complete, here are some items you may think you can deduct, but alas, you can't:

>> Financial planning or investment seminars

>> Any costs connected with attending stockholder meetings

>> Home office expenses for managing your investments

Using Tax-Advantaged Retirement Investing

If you're going to invest for the long term (such as your retirement), you may as well maximize your use of tax-sheltered retirement plans. Many different types of plans are available; I touch on only the most popular ones in the following sections. Although retirement plans may not seem relevant for investors who buy and sell stocks directly (as opposed to a mutual fund), some plans, called *self-directed retirement accounts*, allow you to invest directly.

Individual retirement accounts

IRAs are accounts you can open with a financial institution, such as a bank or a mutual fund company. An IRA is available to almost anyone who has earned income, and it allows you to set aside and invest money to help fund your retirement. Opening an IRA is easy, and virtually any bank or mutual fund can guide you through the process. Two basic types of IRAs are traditional and Roth.

Traditional IRA

The traditional IRA (also called the *deductible IRA*) was first popularized in the early 1980s. In a traditional IRA, you can make a tax-deductible contribution of up to $6,500 in 2023 (some restrictions apply). Individuals age 50 and older can make additional "catch-up" investments of $1,000. For 2024 and beyond, the limits will be indexed to inflation.

The money can then grow in the IRA unfettered by current taxes because the money isn't taxed until you take it out. Because IRAs are designed for retirement purposes, you can start taking money out of your IRA in the year you turn 59½. (Hmm, that must really disappoint those who want their money in the year they turn 58¾.) The withdrawals at that point are taxed as ordinary income. Fortunately (hopefully?), you'll probably be in a lower tax bracket then, so the tax shouldn't be as burdensome.

REMEMBER

Keep in mind that you're required to start taking distributions from your account when you reach age 70½ (that's gotta be a bummer for those who prefer the age of 71⅞). After that point, you may no longer contribute to a traditional IRA. Again, check with your tax advisor to see how this criterion affects you personally.

If you take out money from an IRA too early, the amount is included in your taxable income, and you may be zapped with a 10 percent penalty. You can avoid the penalty if you have a good reason. The IRS provides a list of reasons in Publication 590-B, "Distributions from Individual Retirement Arrangements (IRAs)."

To put money into an IRA, you must earn income equal to or greater than the amount you're contributing. *Earned income* is money made either as an employee or as a self-employed person. Although traditional IRAs can be great for investors, the toughest part about them is qualifying — they have income limitations and other qualifiers that make them less deductible based on how high your income is. See IRS Publication 590-A, "Contributions to Individual Retirement Arrangements (IRAs)," for more details.

TIP

Wait a minute! If IRAs usually involve mutual funds or bank investments, how does the stock investor take advantage of them? Here's how: Stock investors can open a self-directed IRA with a brokerage firm. This means that you can buy and sell stocks in the account with no taxes on dividends or capital gains. The account is tax-deferred, so you don't have to worry about taxes until you start making withdrawals. Also, many dividend reinvestment plans (DRPs) can be set up as IRAs as well.

Roth IRA

The Roth IRA is a great retirement plan that I wish had existed a long time ago. Here are some ways to distinguish the Roth IRA from the traditional IRA:

>> The Roth IRA provides no tax deduction for contributions.

>> Money in the Roth IRA grows tax-free and can be withdrawn tax-free when you turn 59½.

>> The Roth IRA is subject to early distribution penalties (although there are exceptions). Distributions have to be qualified to be penalty- and tax-free; in other words, make sure that any distribution is within the guidelines set by the IRS (see Publication 590-B).

The maximum contribution per year for Roth IRAs is the same as for traditional IRAs. You can open a self-directed account with a broker as well. (See IRS Publication 590-A for details on qualifying.)

401(k) plans

Company-sponsored 401(k) plans are widely used and very popular. In a 401(k) plan, companies set aside money from their employees' paychecks that employees can use to invest for retirement. Generally, in 2023, you can invest as much as $22,500 of your pretax earned income and have it grow tax-deferred. Those over age 50 can contribute up to $7,500 as a "catch-up" contribution.

Usually, the money is put in mutual funds administered through a mutual fund company or an insurance firm. Although most 401(k) plans aren't self-directed, I mention them in this book for good reason.

Because your money is in a mutual fund that may invest in stocks, take an active role in finding out the mutual funds in which you're allowed to invest. Most plans offer several types of stock mutual funds. Use your growing knowledge about stocks to make more informed choices about your 401(k) plan options. For more information on 401(k) and other retirement plans, check out IRS Publication 560.

If you're an employee, you can also find out more about retirement plans from the U.S. Department of Labor at www.dol.gov.

REMEMBER

Keep in mind that a mutual fund is only as good as what it invests in. Ask the plan administrator some questions about the funds and the types of stocks the plan invests in. Are the stocks defensive or cyclical? Are they growth stocks or income stocks (paying a high dividend)? Are they large cap or small cap? (See Chapter 1 for more about these types of stocks.) If you don't make an informed choice about the investments in your plan, someone else will (such as the plan administrator), and that someone probably doesn't have the same ideas about your money that you do.

4

The Part of Tens

Chapter **15**

Ten Hallmarks of a Great Stock

I n a book like this, the ultimate goal would be to identify the holy grail of stock investing — *the* stock, the kind of stock that, if stocks were people, then Apple, Amazon, Procter & Gamble, and Microsoft would be peasants compared to this king. Yeah, that's the kind of stock that would be the Grand Pooh-Bah of your portfolio! Well, hold your horses.

That stock is likely in heaven's stock market right now, and you have to be firmly planted on terra firma. If you have a stock that has all the following features, back up the truck and get as much as you can (and let me know so I can do the same!).

Seriously, I doubt you'll find a stock with all ten indicators described in this chapter, but a stock with even *half* of them is a super-solid choice. Get a stock with as many indicators as possible, and you likely have a winner.

The Company Has Rising Profits

The very essence of a successful company is its ability to make a profit. In fact, profit is the single most important financial element of a company. I can even make the case that profit is the single most important element of a successful economy. Without profit, a company goes out of business. If a business closes its doors, private jobs vanish. In turn, taxes don't get paid. This means that the government can't function and pay its workers and those who are dependent on public assistance. Sorry for veering away from the company's main hallmark, but understanding the importance of profit is vital.

REMEMBER

Profit is what is left after expenses are deducted from sales. When a company manages its expenses well, profits grow. (For info on the numbers measuring a company's success, turn to Chapters 5 and 6.)

The Company Has Rising Sales

Looking at the total sales of a company is referred to as analyzing the *top-line numbers*. Of course, that's because when you're looking at net income (gross sales minus total expenses), you're looking at the bottom line.

A company (or analysts) can play games with many numbers on an income statement; there are a dozen different ways to look at earnings. Earnings are the heart and soul of a company, but the top line gives you an unmistakable and clear number to look at. The total sales (or gross sales or gross revenue) number for a company is harder to fudge.

TIP

It's easy for an investor — especially a novice investor — to look at sales for a company for a particular year and see whether it's doing better or worse than in the prior year. Reviewing three years of sales gives you a good overall gauge of the company's success.

Granted, some years are bad for everyone, so don't expect a company's sales to go up every year like a rocket. Sometimes success is relative; a company with sales down 5 percent is doing fine if every other company in that industry has sales down much more.

Suffice it to say that when a company's total sales are rising, that's a positive sign. The company can overcome other potential issues (such as paying off debt or sudden expenses) much more easily and can pave the way for long-term success.

The Company Has Low Liabilities

All things being equal, I would rather have a company with relatively low debt than one with high debt. Too much debt can kill an otherwise good company. Debt can consume you, and as you read this, debt is consuming many countries across the globe.

Because a company with low debt has borrowing power, it can take advantage of opportunities such as taking over a rival or acquiring a company that offers an added technology to help propel current or future profit growth.

Notice that I didn't say a company with no debt. Don't get me wrong — a company with no debt or little in the way of liabilities is a solid company. But in an environment where you can borrow at historically low rates, it pays to take on some debt and use it efficiently. In other words, if a company can borrow at, say, 3 percent and put it to use to yield a profit of 5 percent or more, why not?

REMEMBER

Notice that I'm talking about liabilities. It isn't always conventional debt that may sink a company. What if that company is simply spending more money than it's bringing in? Liabilities or "total liabilities" takes into account everything that a company is obligated to pay, whether it's a long-term bond (long-term debt), paying workers, or the water bill. Current expenses should be more than covered by current income, but you don't want to accumulate long-term debt, which means a drain on future income.

Also, in some industries, the liabilities can take a form that isn't typically conventional debt or monthly expenses. I read a recent industry report that some very large banks and stock brokerage firms have huge positions in *derivatives*, which are complicated financial instruments that can easily turn into crushing debt that could sink a bank.

In my research, for example, I found one Wall Street broker that had total derivatives of a whopping $35 trillion, even though its net worth on its balance sheet was only $104 billion. There is actually an agency that tracks these numbers — the Office of the Comptroller of the Currency (www.occ.treas.gov). You should check it out when you're considering investing in these types of financial institutions.

The point is that one of the hallmarks of a successful company is to keep liabilities low and manageable. You can find a company's debt in its financial statements, such as the balance sheet. (Find out more about debt in Chapter 6.)

The Stock Is at a Bargain Price

Price and value are two different concepts, and they aren't interchangeable. A low price isn't synonymous with a bargain. Just as you want to get the most for your money when you shop, you want to get the most for your money when you invest in stocks.

You can look at the value of a company in several ways, but the first thing I look at is the price-to-earnings ratio (P/E ratio). It attempts to connect the price of the company's stock to the company's net profits quoted on a per-share basis. For example, if a company has a price of $15 per share, and the earnings are $1 per share, then the P/E ratio is 15.

REMEMBER

Generally speaking, a P/E ratio of 15 or less is a good value, especially if the other numbers work out positively (for example, profits and sales are rising, as I note earlier in this chapter). When the economy is in the dumps and stock prices are down, P/E ratios of 10 or lower are even better. Conversely, if the economy is booming, higher P/E ratios are acceptable.

I consider myself a value investor, so P/E ratios in the teens or lower make me comfortable. However, someone else may bristle at that and consider P/E ratios of 25 or even 50 acceptable. Then again, at those levels (or higher), you're no longer talking about a bargain. Just keep in mind that when stocks have much higher P/E ratios (such as 75, 100, and beyond), it means that stock investors have high expectations for the company's earnings; if the earnings don't materialize, the risk is that the stock will tumble, so be wary of high P/E ratios.

WARNING

Too many investors see no problem with buying stocks that have no P/E ratio. These stocks may have the P (price of the stock), but they have no E (earnings). If you invest in a company that has losses instead of earnings, then to me you aren't an investor; you're a speculator.

Investing in a company that's losing money is making a bet, and more important, it isn't a bargain at all. (However, when you find a company that's losing money, it could be a good shorting opportunity; see Chapter 13 for details.)

A stock may also be a bargain if its market value is at or below its *book value* (the actual accounting value of net assets for the company). (You can find out more about book value in Chapter 6.)

Dividends Are Growing

Long-term investing is where the true payoff is for today's investors. But before you start staring at your calendar and dreaming of future profits, take a look at the company's current dividend picture.

Dividends are the long-term investor's best friend. Wouldn't it be great if after a few years of owning that stock, you received total dividends that actually dwarfed what your original investment was? That's more common than you know! I've calculated the history of accumulated dividends for a given stock, and it doesn't take as long as you think to get your original investment amount back (counting cumulated dividends). I know some people who bought dividend-paying stocks during a bear market (when stock prices are very low) and got their original investment back after eight to ten years (depending on the stock and its dividend growth, of course).

Dividend growth also carries with it the potential growth of the stock itself. A consistently rising dividend is a positive sign for the stock price. The investing public sees that a growing dividend is a powerful and tangible sign of the company's current and future financial health.

A company may be able to fudge earnings and other soft or malleable figures, but when a dividend is paid, that's hard proof that the company is succeeding with its net profit. Given that, just review the long-term stock chart (say, five years or longer) of a consistent dividend-paying company, and 99 times out of 100, that stock price is zigzagging upward in a similar pattern.

I discuss dividends and dividend-growing stocks in Chapter 10. For exchange-traded funds (ETFs) that have dividend stocks in their portfolios, see Chapter 11.

The Market Is Growing

In this context, when I say that the market is growing, I mean the market of consumers for a given product. If more and more people are buying widgets (remember those?) and the sales of widgets keep growing, that bodes well for companies that sell (or service) widgets.

Take a look at demographics and market data, and use this information to further filter your investing choices. You could run a great company, but if your fortunes are made when a million folks buy from you, and next year that number shrinks to 800,000, and the year after that it shrinks again, what will happen to your fortunes?

Consider this example: If you have a successful company that's selling something to seniors, and the market data tells you that the number of seniors is expanding relentlessly for the foreseeable future, then this rising tide (demographics) will certainly lift that particular boat (your stock).

The Company Is in a Field with a High Barrier to Entry

If you run a company that offers a product or service that is easy to compete with, building up a strong and viable business will be more difficult for you; you'll need to do something different and better.

Maybe you have a great technology, or a patented system, or superior marketing prowess, or a way to make what you're selling both cheaper and faster than your competition. Maybe you have a strong brand that has endured for decades.

A *high barrier to entry* simply means that companies that compete with you will have a tough time overcoming your advantage. This gives you the power to grow and leave your competition in the dust.

Here's an example: Coca-Cola positioned and branded itself for decades as the top soda with a secret recipe for its soda. In spite of imitators and competitors, it's still dominant today — more than a century after its founding. The company's soda is still on kitchen tables and in picnic baskets, and its shareholders are still being refreshed with stock splits and dividend increases.

The Company Has a Low Political Profile

Politics: Just the thought of it makes me wince. Political discussions may be great at cocktail parties and perhaps fun to watch as your relatives go at it, but I think flying below the political radar is a good thing for companies.

Why? We live in times that are politically sensitive (I don't think that is a good thing). All too often, politics affects the fortunes of companies and, by extension, the portfolios of investors. Yes, sometimes politics can favor a company (through backroom deals and such), but politics is a double-edged sword that can ruin a company.

History shows us that companies that are politically targeted either directly or by association (by being in an unpopular industry) can suffer. There was a time that holding tobacco companies in your portfolio was the equivalent of garlic to a vampire.

REMEMBER

All things being equal, I would rather hold a stock in a popular industry or a nondescript industry than one that attracts undue (negative) attention.

The Stock Is Optionable

An *optionable stock* (which has call and put options available on it) gives you more ways to profit from it (or the ability to minimize potential losses). Options give a stockholder ways to enhance gains or yield added revenue.

Say you do, in fact, find the perfect stock, and you truly load up and buy as many shares as you can lay your hands on, but you don't have any more money to buy another batch of shares.

Fortunately, you notice that the stock is optionable and see that you can speculate by buying a call option that allows you to be bullish on 100 shares with a fraction of the cash needed to actually buy 100 shares. As the stock soars, you're able to take profits by cashing out the call option without having to touch the stock position at all.

Now, with your stock at nosebleed levels, you're getting a little nervous that this stock is possibly at an unsustainable level, so you decide to buy some put options to protect your unrealized gains from your stock. When your stock does experience a correction, you cash out your put with an enviable gain. With the stock down, you decide to take the proceeds from your put option–realized gains and buy more of the stock at favorable prices.

TIP

Options (both the call and the put in this scenario) give you the ability to bank more gains from the same great stock. Just keep in mind that options are a speculative vehicle and can expire. Find out more about options in my book *High-Level Investing For Dummies* (Wiley).

The Stock Is Benefiting from Favorable Megatrends

A *megatrend* is a trend that affects an unusually large segment of the marketplace and may have added benefits and/or pitfalls for buyers and sellers of a given set of products and services. A good example of a megatrend is "the aging of America"; the United States has more than 85 million people who are getting ready for retirement as they reach and surpass the age of 65 (although some assume a larger number when they include folks who are over 50). Companies that provide services and products for senior citizens will have greater opportunities to sell more of what they provide and will then be a good consideration for investors.

REMEMBER

When megatrends are with you, you can even have a mediocre stock but end up with extraordinary gains. In fact, even a "bad" stock will rise sharply if it's swept up in a rally pushed by a powerful megatrend. Of course, a bad stock won't have staying power (the stock will eventually go down if the underlying company is losing money or struggling), so stick to quality stocks to truly optimize the long-term benefits that a megatrend can provide.

The problem is that when a stock has little substance behind it (the company is losing money, growing debt, and so on), its up move will be temporary, and the stock price will tend to reverse in an ugly pullback. Just ask anyone who bought a dot-com stock from 1999 to 2001 (that's right — the person softly sobbing in the corner). The rising-tide-lifts-all-boats idea is a powerful one, and when you have a great company that will only benefit from this type of scenario, your stock price will go higher and higher.

Find out more about megatrends and other factors in the big picture in Chapter 12.

Chapter **16**

Ten Investment Strategies That Work Well with Stocks

Y es, I love stocks, and I think some type of stock exposure is good for virtually any portfolio. But you must remember that your total financial portfolio should have other investments and strategies that are not stocks at all. Why?

Diversification means you have other assets besides stocks so you're not 100 percent tied to the whims and machinations of the stock market. All too often, too many investors have too much exposure to the stock market. That's fine, of course, when the stock market is raging upward, but potential down moves are there, too. For this reason, you should consider investments and strategies that complement your stock-investing pursuits. Check out ten of my favorites in this chapter.

Covered Call Options

Writing a covered call option is a great strategy for generating income from a current stock position (or positions) in your portfolio. A *call option* is a vehicle that gives the call buyer the right (but not the obligation) to buy a particular stock at a given price during a limited time frame (call options expire). The buyer pays what's called the *premium* to the call seller (referred to as the *call writer*). The call writer receives the premium as income but in return is obligated to sell the stock to the buyer at the agreed-upon price (called the *strike price*) if called upon to do so during the life of the option. The call option is typically a speculative vehicle for those who are buying them, but in this case I specifically refer to writing a covered call option.

Covered call writing is a conservative way to make extra cash from just about any listed stock of which you own at least 100 shares. Whether your stock has a dividend or not, this could boost income by 5 percent or more.

To find out more about writing call options on your stock positions, check out my book *High-Level Investing For Dummies* (Wiley). There you'll find several chapters detailing the basics of options, along with their advantages and disadvantages. I also discuss writing covered calls in Chapter 10 of this book.

Put Options

A *put option* is a bet that a stock or exchange-traded fund (ETF) will fall in price. If you see the fortunes of a company going down, a put option is a great way to make a profit by speculating that the stock will go down. Many investors use puts to speculate for a profit, while others use put options as a hedging vehicle or a form of "portfolio insurance."

TIP

If you're holding a stock for the long term but you're concerned about it in the short term, then consider using a put option on that stock. You're not hoping the stock goes down; you're merely using a form of protection for your stock holding. If the stock goes down, the put option will rise in value. What some investors do is then cash out the put option at a profit, and use the proceeds to buy more shares of that stock because the stock's price is lower and possibly a buying opportunity.

For more on put options, see my book *High-Level Investing For Dummies* (Wiley).

Cash

Having some money in the bank or just some cash in your brokerage account comes in handy no matter what's happening with the stock market's gyrations. What's that? The stock market is plunging? Whew! Good to have some cash on the sidelines so you can do some bargain hunting for good value stocks.

REMEMBER

When interest rates on savings accounts and similar bank vehicles are abysmally low, cash isn't a great investment. However, cash is an integral part of your overall wealth-building approach for several reasons:

>> Cash you hold on the sidelines (either at your bank or, more conveniently, in your stock brokerage account or money-market fund) is necessary when buying opportunities present themselves during the ebbs and flows of the stock market.

>> Cash is necessary for an emergency fund in your overall financial-planning picture. Not enough folks have an emergency or "rainy day" fund, which means a hundred different things (big medical expense, job layoff, and so on) could cause them a cash flow problem. If you need money for an unexpected big expense and you don't have it in savings (or under your mattress!), where will that money come from? It's a good possibility that you'd have to sell or cash out some investment (such as your stock). (See Chapter 2 for more about emergency funds.)

>> Cash can be necessary when you're doing an income strategy referred to as *writing puts* because a put may mean having to buy a stock or ETF. (You can find more on writing puts in Chapter 10.)

>> Cash is a good holding during deflationary times. When prices are low or going down, your cash's buying power gets stronger.

EE Savings Bonds

The EE savings bond is issued by the U.S. Treasury and is a great vehicle, especially for small investors (you can buy one for as little as $25). It's a discount bond, meaning that you buy it at below its face value (the purchase price is 50 percent of the face value), and cash it in later to get your purchase price back with interest.

The interest rate paid is equivalent to 100 percent of the average five-year Treasury note rate. If this rate is at 2 percent, you get 2 percent. To get the full benefit of the rate, you must hold your EE bond for at least five years. If you cash out before five years but after one year (the mandatory minimum holding period), you get a lower interest rate (equivalent to a savings account rate).

Here are several benefits of an EE bond:

>> The interest rate isn't fixed. Because the rate is pegged to Treasury note interest rates, it will rise (or fall) along with that rate. In the event that interest rates rise, EE bonds would benefit.

>> The interest you earn on EE bonds is typically higher than a conventional bank account.

>> EE bonds are free from state and local taxes. If you use the bonds for education, much of the interest can be tax-free.

TIP

For more details on the EE savings bond, head over to the U.S. Treasury's site on savings bonds (`https://treasurydirect.gov/savings-bonds`).

I Bonds

In the age of low-interest-rate debt investments (such as bonds in general), the I savings bond (the *I* stands for *inflation*) is a different wrinkle altogether. This is a "sister" to the EE savings bond (see the preceding section), and it's also issued by the U.S. Treasury. The twist here (making it a "twisted sister," I guess) is that the interest rate is tied to the official inflation rate (the Consumer Price Index, or CPI). If the CPI goes to 3 percent, the interest rate on the I bond goes to 3 percent. The interest rate is adjusted annually.

As I write this in 2023, inflation is an issue for consumers and investors, and the I Bond continues to be a good consideration as part of a diversified portfolio. The nominal rate on an I bond was 6.89 percent as of April 2023. Not bad!

TIP

Having savings bonds (I bonds or EE bonds) as tools in your investing arsenal can be a good complement to your stock-investing pursuits. Get the full details on them at `https://treasurydirect.gov/savings-bonds`.

Sector Mutual Funds

I think that sector investing is a great part of your overall wealth-building approach; sometimes it isn't easy to choose a single stock, but you can instead choose a winning sector (or industry). For many investors, a sector mutual fund is a good addition to their portfolios.

A *mutual fund* is a pool of money that's managed by an investment firm (such as Fidelity, Vanguard, or T. Rowe Price); this pool of money is invested in a portfolio of securities (such as stocks or bonds) to reach a particular objective (such as aggressive growth, income, or preservation of capital). The investment firm actively manages the fund by regularly making buy, sell, and hold decisions in the fund's portfolio.

A sector mutual fund limits its portfolio and investment decisions to a particular sector, such as utilities, consumer staples, or health care. Your task is to choose a winning sector, and the job of choosing the various stocks is left to the investment firm. (Turn to Chapter 12 for details on sectors and industries.)

Physical Gold and Silver

As I write this in 2023, paper assets have been very vulnerable to losses. We're watching the issues of trillion-dollar spending culminating in dangerous bubbles in the world of debt, bonds, and currencies. Wise investors understand the benefits of diversification, especially away from the inherent risks of paper assets.

Given that, keep an important concept in mind: counter-party risk. All paper assets in the world of investing have counter-party risk. *Counter-party risk* means that the value of a given paper asset (such as stocks, bonds, or currencies) is only as safe as the promise or guarantee of the counter-party involved. If you loan money to someone (such as putting money in a bank account or buying a bond), that money is only as safe as the entity guaranteeing the return of your money (and any promised interest). If you buy a bond and the bond issuer (government agency, corporation, and so on) defaults and doesn't pay you your principal and interest (such as in a bankruptcy), then your bond can become worthless. What's that? You own stock? If the underlying company goes bankrupt, your stock can become worthless, too.

So, what's an investor to do? Physical gold and silver don't have counter-party risk, so adding them to your portfolio means diversifying away from counter-party risk.

For more information, check out my book *Investing in Gold & Silver For Dummies* (Wiley).

Bearish Exchange-Traded Funds

The tumult of domestic politics and geopolitics looms due to general economic weakness, unsustainable debt, political upheaval, and global economic and financial difficulties. What should investors do, given those possible scenarios?

Investors can do plenty of things, both before and during tumultuous market times. If you're invested in quality stocks, you shouldn't panic, especially if you have a long-term outlook. But hedging to a small extent can be a good consideration. In other words, why not consider a vehicle that will benefit in the event of a downturn in the stock market?

ETFs are a good companion vehicle in your stock portfolio, and their versatility can become part of your overall strategy. If you believe that the stock market is or soon will be in difficult times, consider a bearish stock market ETF. A bearish (or inverse) stock ETF is designed to go up when stocks go down. If stocks go down

5 percent, the bearish ETF goes up by a similar inverse percentage (in this case, 5 percent).

TIP

What some investors do with bearish ETFs is cash them out when the market plunges and then take the proceeds to buy more of their favorite stocks (which presumably are cheaper given the market's move down). Tactics such as this mean you keep your portfolio growing for the long term while playing it safe during short-term market difficulties. (Turn to Chapter 11 for general information on ETFs.)

Dividend Yield Exchange-Traded Funds

The movement of stock prices can certainly be puzzling at times. Because they're subject to buying and selling orders, their movement may not always be logical or predictable, especially in the short term (and I mean especially!). There is, however, one aspect of stocks that is much more logical and predictable: dividends.

Strong, profitable companies that have consistently raised their dividends in the past tend to reliably keep doing so in the future. Many companies have raised their dividends, or at the very least, kept paying them, year in and year out, through good times and bad. Dividends are paid out from the company's net earnings (or net profit), so dividends also tend to act as a barometer for gauging the company's financial health, which basically boils down to profitability.

TIP

Finding good dividend-paying stocks isn't hard (see Chapter 10). However, investing in a strong basket of dividend-paying stocks by checking out dividend yield ETFs can be a good idea — especially for those who are too skittish to invest in individual stocks. A dividend yield ETF selects a basket of stocks based on the criteria of dividends — how consistently they're paid and continuously raised. They make it easy to include dividend payers in your portfolio with a single purchase. (I cover ETFs in more detail in Chapter 11.)

Consumer Staples Exchange-Traded Funds

REMEMBER

You should consider having investments in your portfolio that are *defensive* in nature — investments tied to those products and services that people will keep buying no matter how good or bad the economy is. Sure, consider that sexy, high-tech gizmo stock if you like, but offset that with stocks of companies that offer food, beverages, water, utilities, and so on. However, sometimes it isn't easy to find that one great defensive stock, so why not buy the sector?

The consumer staples sector includes the "old reliables" of stock investing. Consumer staples ETFs may not skyrocket during bull markets (although they'll perform respectably), but they'll forge ahead during bad or uncertain times. Fortunately, the world of ETFs has made it a snap to invest in a basket of stocks that generally mirror a given sector. (I discuss ETFs in Chapter 11 and sectors in Chapter 12.)

Index

About the Author

Paul Mladjenovic is a national speaker, educator, and best-selling author. He was a Certified Financial Planner (CFP) for 36 years (1985–2021). Since launching his business in 1981, he has specialized in investing, financial planning, and home business issues. During those nearly four decades, he has helped hundreds of thousands of students and readers build wealth through his nationwide seminars, workshops, conferences, and coaching program.

Besides this book, Paul has written all editions of *Stock Investing For Dummies*, *Investing in Gold & Silver For Dummies*, *Factor Investing For Dummies* (coauthor), *High-Level Investing For Dummies*, *Micro-Entrepreneurship For Dummies*, *Zero-Cost Marketing*, *Precious Metals Investing For Dummies*, and *The Job Hunter's Encyclopedia*. In 2019, he coauthored *Affiliate Marketing For Dummies*. His national (and online) seminars include "The $50 Wealth-Builder," "Ultra-Investing with Options," and the "Home Business Goldmine," among others. The full details on his (downloadable) financial and business start-up audio seminars can be found at www.ravingcapitalist.com. His online courses can also be found at educational venues such as Udemy (www.udemy.com), Skillshare (www.skillshare.com), Colorado Free University (www.freeu.com), and Mt. Airy Learning Tree (https://mtairylearningtree.org).

Since 2000, Paul has built a reputation as an accurate economics and market forecaster. His long record includes accurate forecasts of the housing bubble, the energy crisis, the Great Recession, the rise of precious metals, and much more. He has been interviewed or referenced by numerous media sources, such as Comcast, CNN, MarketWatch, Bloomberg, OANN, Fox Business, *Futures* magazine, Kitco, GoldSeek, Investopedia, Minyanville, Financial Sense, PreciousMetalsInvesting.com, and other media venues.

You can view Paul's profile at www.linkedin.com/in/paul mladjenovic and you can also check out his page at www.amazon.com/author/paulmladjenovic. Paul invites readers to send questions or inquiries directly to paul@mladjenovic.com or via the bio page at www.ravingcapitalist.com.

Dedication

I send my appreciation and gratitude to those who helped me make this a reality. I wish you, my audience, a successful and prosperous future!

Author's Acknowledgments

First and foremost, I offer my appreciation and gratitude to the wonderful folks at Wiley. It has been a pleasure to work with such a top-notch organization that works so hard to create products that offer readers tremendous value and information. I wish all of you continued success!

In particular, with deep and joyful gratitude, I thank Tracy Boggier, my superb acquisitions editor. Thank you so much for being my champion at Wiley and shepherding yet another *For Dummies* guide for me to author, and I can't express enough appreciation for all that you do. *For Dummies* books are great, and they appear on your bookshelf only through the planning and professional efforts of publishing pros like Tracy.

I am grateful to my book agents, Sheree Bykofsky and Janet Rosen, two of the best pros on the planet! Their guidance and assistance made this book (and many others) arrive in the Wiley universe, and I appreciate all that they do.

Fran, Lipa Zyenska, thank you and my boys, Adam and Joshua, with all my heart for your support and being my number-one fans throughout the writing of this book. I am grateful to have you by my side always! I thank God for you, and I love you beyond words!

Lastly, I want to acknowledge you, the reader. Over the years, you've made the *For Dummies* series the popular and indispensable books they are today. Thank you, and I wish you continued success!

Publisher's Acknowledgments

Senior Acquisitions Editor:
Tracy Boggier

Senior Managing Editor:
Kristie Pyles

Compilation Editor:
Georgette Beatty

Editor: Elizabeth Kuball

Production Editor:
Saikarthick Kumarasamy

Cover Images:
Frame: © aleksandarvelasevic/
Getty Images
Paper texture: © Dmitr1ch/
Getty Images
Inset: © 13ree_design/
Adobe Stock